MEETING THE MONKEY HALFWAY

MEETING
THEMONKEY
HALFWAY

AJAHN SUMANO BHIKKHU
WITH EMILY POPP

SAMUEL WEISER, INC.

York Beach, Maine

First published in 2000 by
Samuel Weiser, Inc.
P.O. Box 612
York Beach, ME 03910-0612
www.weiserbooks.com

Library of Congress Cataloging-in-Publication Data
Ajahn Sumano, Bhikkhu.
    Meeting the monkey halfway / Ajahn Sumano
Bhikkhu.
      p. cm.
    ISBN 1-57863-146-7 (pbk. : alk. paper)
    1. Religious life—Buddhism. 2. Buddhism—
Doctrines. I. Title.
    BQ4302 .A37 2000
    294.3'444—dc21
                                        99–058179
BJ

Typeset in 10.5/14 Optima with Ragged as a display face.
Printed in the United States of America

Cover photograph by Jane Smith, used by kind permission.

07 06 05 04 03 02 01 00
8 7 6 5 4 3 2 1

The paper used in this publication meets the minimum
requirements of the American National Standard for
Information Sciences—Permanence of Paper for Printed
Library Materials Z39.48-1992 (R1997).

CONTENTS

Contents

FOREWORD

In the ancient wisdom teachings of Asia, the monkey is a symbol of a mind that bounces capriciously from one activity to another—restless, wayward, and unsettled. It is this "monkey mind" that Eastern spiritual training exercises, such as meditation, yoga, and mantra chanting, attempt to bring under control.

"Halfway" expresses the wise approach we must take in dealing with the mind—one that comes with neither too much ambition or too little flexibility; one that doesn't waver with indecision and wishy-washy intentions. "Halfway" is the attitude of perfect balance that remains untouched by the comings and goings of the monkey mind.

"Meeting" connotes a dynamic effort toward a subject or a goal. It implies an enthusiastic, resolute movement to stabilize the irrepressible mind that cannot retain a moment's peace. This determined effort, applied with diligence and integrity, and directed by wisdom, will enable us to acquire the discipline required to get us on the right track, so that we can "meet the monkey halfway."

PREFACE

The world is full of confused people running around aimlessly, waiting for life to happen. Caught in a maze of mirrors, they spend most of their time bumping into walls of confusion and chaos that we who inhabit this world have created.

In attempting to find remedies for the ailments of the world, we first have to look for the cause of this situation. Does the problem lie with and within the world? The world is just being what it is: the world. The problem lies not with the world, but with our attitude toward it. The world is a changeable factor and it is this aspect that spins us about in all directions without our being aware of our center. Every now and then, a spark of intuitive instinct slips through that somehow enables us to function automatically in the shadow of reality. While we recognize that there is some degree of convenience to that mode of living, in the long run, we notice that something is essentially wrong with it. Viewed from a detached dimension, it is tasteless and dry. This is the gigantic downside of our chronic misperception.

In terms of Buddhist reality, we have been swallowed up by our ego-I, which determines our relationship with the world. We are left to dangle on strings, like marionettes. Our egos try everything to preserve our fantasy roles and identities in order to maintain the status quo.

There are many different kinds of knowledge in this world, many different dimensions of truth. The ego-I should really mostly concern itself with survival, but instead it has usurped a much larger role in our lives than it should. It is most troublesome when it intrudes in matters of significance, in the deeper spiritual issues.

A LITTLE SPIRITUAL BOOK

The highest knowledge is really the background lighting or the continual awareness that can direct our life in a way that shines and showers dignity to our birth as a human being.

This little book presents perspectives from the Buddha's view of the world. It is offered as a remedial treatment. Just as medicines are intended to deal with dysfunction, illness, and injury, so this spiritual path is meant to serve as a tool to make our hearts well, to bring radiating peace into our hearts. This is the heart that is settled into its natural home.

The Buddha, like all spiritual masters and saints, offered medicines that help open the heart, enhance perspectives, stretch attitudes into new territories, radiate loving-kindness, and reveal our true compassionate nature. This is our natural state when our mind is not obstructed by fear and selfish concerns.

Your awareness of truth in itself is a powerful form of energy that can actively participate in elevating the world to a new level of awareness. This is the most powerful energy we can access. Such benevolent energy offers a sharp contrast to the usual, devious inner directives used in fueling the engine of our personal chaotic world.

This book attempts to address only the sublime truth that transcends all worldly matters. It is not a primer offering clever advice on how to handle life's inconveniences or suggestions on how to get a good deal on a car, on international banking, or outwit the tax authorities! We can leave that for the financial advisors on the upper floors of major corporations in every big city.

As a spiritual instruction book, it goes far deeper into the very heart of our lives. It offers all of us a collective understanding of the world as it really is, so that we can use the energy that comes from a unified heart and mind to influence the course of things in this world in a meaningful way. This is absolutely true: We are beings with reflective consciousness. That means that, even individually, we possess enormous power, a power sufficient to significantly change the world. We are really reluctant to acknowledge this fact because we have been so heavily conditioned to believe that the world changes through political and economic factors. The world can never be made significantly better through political maneuvering. Real progress can only be brought about by the infusion of a deepened sense of our spiritual life that softens and opens the heart. The path of wisdom and compassion is the way of peaceful, beneficial evolution.

A spiritual instruction book should strive to be simple and straightforward. Its single intent must be to be in the moment, in the real life that is happening, right here and now.

This "little book" is a distillation of almost twenty years of meditation practice as a Buddhist monk. The opportunity to practice meditation as a monk has been a great blessing, one that has been supported by everyone and everything in the world, consciously or unconsciously. As a grateful recipient of this generosity, I have an obligation and responsibility to bear witness only to the universal truth. To honor both of these aspects, I am concentrating on that which matters most to the evolution of the human life.

We need not preoccupy ourselves with petty, inconsequential matters, nor waste time planning elaborate schemes just to survive this complex world. None of us need lose sleep over birthdays, anniversaries, or other trivial events. None of us need make life more interesting by scouting out white sales, demanding every inch of our legal rights, or sniffing out bargains at the flea market. We are not called to do that. By abandoning these frivolous adventures, we allow ourselves more space to live a spontaneous and free life. Then we will have room to leap for joy within. Life is now! It is important for us to learn how to live in an appropriate manner—moderately, with a sense of reverence and respect for everything. We must learn to use only what we need, and then to use these few things carefully and with discrimination. With wisdom and compassion we respond appropriately to life. We can do this only when our minds are on our hearts. We are here to *live*.

This book is intended to awaken a realization that the world is not perceived solely through the lens of conditioning and habit. It is not intended to encourage others to be overly assertive, obstinate, or willful.

Some so-called spiritual books seem to guide people toward a stand-your-ground attitude rather than to appeal to their loftier nature. Anything genuinely spiritual must be related to compassion. And compassion arises out of wisdom, the all-seeing eye of mindful awareness in the now, the open, empty eye that is clear, fresh, and creative.

This book seeks to steer your interest toward an assortment of skillful thoughts and mental formations, so that you can understand how to avoid all suffering and be free of it.

INTRODUCTION

Nowadays, bookstore shelves are crammed with all kinds of "little" life-instruction books. These mini-books are presented as primers that offer advice on how to make life more interesting and stimulating. They make for light enjoyable reading because they give whimsical, folksy advice that speaks to the common experiences most of us come across in our daily lives. Every now and then, they may even carry a nugget or two of wisdom and end up as favorite quotable quotes tacked on someone's refrigerator door. Their flippant, down-home approach to living is quickly becoming the modern bible of this generation. Although the advice in these books is sometimes astute, sometimes clever, and often humorous, they rarely ever reach into profundity. Here are some of the interesting topics I have come across at airports and train station bookstores:

* The Quintessential Smart Shopper
* How to Survive an IRS Audit
* Applied Chutzpah: Staring Down the World
* Pointers on Tipping with Sensitivity
* Around the World on Air-Mileage Tickets
* Meditation for those Winning Numbers
* Forever Young

The intention behind most of these mini-books is to offer useful, effective, time-tested ways of coping with our daily travails in a confused and chaotic world. I believe that they offer a sincere effort to represent some good old-fashioned values that may very well have been quoted from Granny's book of wisdom.

Generally, however, these values don't go deep enough to leave a lasting impression on anyone. They seem to be right, but not quite right enough, often just lacking that significant aspect that calls for the application of basic virtues. And yet, given the popularity of such books, I have to wonder if this is how far most of us are willing to go to preserve the sanctity of our "souls." Is a minute a day all the time we are willing to invest in trying to understand our spiritual destiny? Surely there must be a handful out there who are ready to go the distance for a glimpse of the possibilities beyond this life. It is for the benefit of those spiritually curious minds that I address my insights and share my version of the "little book."

These several pages have been drawn from a distillation of twenty years or so of my practice as a Buddhist monk—although, having said that, I can not overlook the cathartic experiences of my pre-monastic life that have brought me to where I am now. From those tender, impressionable years spent in the company of my grandfather, a highly respected rabbi in our neighborhood, to my teenage pursuits of amateur boxing, bowling, and books written by revolutionary thinkers (Alan Watts, Christmas Humphreys, and D. T. Suzuki), to my career-crazed years as a wheeling-dealing real estate mogul—all of these phases and experiences in my ordinary life have led me to the epiphany that finally drove me to this cave where I now sit in silence.

MEETING
THE MONKEY
HALFWAY

Meditation and the Mind

Understanding the Relationship Between the Two

❖

The mind is malleable and transformable. Though we don't really know much about its nature and essence, we still have to be involved with it, or be it, in whatever capacity we can. We will describe this situation differently, depending on our perceptions and understanding.

Investigating the mind, however, requires the use of the very thing we want to study. The mind functions as both the subject and object in this case. In a conventional sense, this limits us to a superficial understanding, possibly coupled with a glimpse of some deeper aspects in the mind (or qualities of mind) that we recognize only through intuition. The superficiality is locked in by our descriptive language that attaches labels to the surface of things, preventing a meaningful exploration of either subject or object.

Meditation is the entering into this process. It allows us to penetrate the barrier of chaotic language, taking us beyond rationality and placing our mind's eye beyond the influence of the intellect.

The inner world of meditation is truly the essence of mind. It is here that the quality of mind can be transformed in profound ways, not just altered or rearranged (as in many therapies). Meditation requires a deliberate, determined intention to transform the mind in the direction of its natural, unconditioned state—a state we call enlightenment.

As awesome as this word may seem, it is without actual substance and ultimately empty. Emptiness as a spiritual goal, however, does not inspire transformational zeal in people. Translators have wisely chosen the word *enlightenment* to describe the "original mind," one that has divested itself of every obstacle in reaching the light of consciousness.

This process of purification occurs naturally through meditation. It is the pure intention behind our efforts that initiates the rebalancing that, in turn, prompt the mind to regain its original stability. In its original state, the balanced mind is no longer enslaved by unskillful habits and inclinations. It abides in the present moment, awake and alert.

Nothing significant comes easily. To reach anything profound, you must start with the courage to explore. You will always face the risks that come with running against the common grain. If you are willing to make this effort, the meditative affirmations given in the following chapters can gradually transform your mind in the direction of peace and harmony. It is possible to attain peace. The natural tendency to seek it is inherent in our nature.

In this type of endeavor, only the actual "doing" counts. Thinking or reading about mental cultivation won't get you very far. As you work with these affirmations, your mind will naturally develop more courage, spontaneity, happiness, and maturity, and a sense of the possibilities toward which you are already inclined.

People who have dedicated their lives to this practice are poised to get beyond the reach of suffering, conflict, loneliness, and confusion. At the end of it all, the bliss in their hearts far surpasses all the fleeting pleasures of sex, rock and roll, drugs, alcohol, and romance. That's not to say that these activities aren't pleasurable and fun. They certainly can be. They are, however, hopeless pursuits that cannot deliver lasting happiness. They are all too brief and invariably not quite good enough.

In the conventional world of description and definition, we can only interpret the surface of things as they manifest through our senses. We are limited to words themselves, and words only allow us access to reality in mental terms.

Spiritual practice looks intuitively behind the visible, into the core essence that manifests itself in the world. When you recognize that you can come to that inner reality, you also realize that it is the nature of this consciousness that creates your inner world as images. These images arise spontaneously and flow out from an inner force—unknowable and indescribable to your limited, rational consciousness.

Since this inner force creates your world, and since it can be connected to intuitively, you can shape the character and quality of your world by transforming this inner force. It is malleable, flexible, and trainable. You can train it through contemplation. This technique is called "working with affirmations."

SOFTENING AND STRETCHING AFFIRMATIONS

❖

Growing and sustaining wisdom-awareness in these ultramodern times require a response based on grounded spirituality. As we try to keep our heads above the flood of information, data, and messages inundating us each second, we are faced with the choice of making this situation work to our advantage or allowing the deluge to overwhelm us. Our spiritual survival is threatened by the sheer volume of superficial trivia. We risk drowning our intuition and spiritual nature in a sea of meaningless jargon.

To reclaim the ground lost to the Information Age, I offer you a series of potent spiritual messages that I have gathered with great care over many years of practice. You might call this offering an insight buffet or, simply, a wisdom banquet.

These reflections on wisdom have been a part of the perennial wisdom of the East—Buddhist dharma practice—for thousands of years. They have been utilized to great advantage by meditators, yogis, and saints since the dawn of intelligence. They represent a common thread of understanding shared by Buddhism, Hinduism, Sufism, and Taoism.

The essence of all perennial wisdom is the understanding that the major source of human suffering comes through wrong thought. When these unskillful thoughts are translated into action, they cause the conflicts and delusion that bring about suffering and pain. If you want to change your actions, you must necessarily change the way you relate to thoughts, for thought is the mother of action.

With this understanding clearly established in your mind, you can use skillful spiritual reflections to replace unskillful thoughts. In Pali, this is called "oobai," or skillful means. Through the persistent application of oobai, you can significantly alter the way you live and give your life more profound meaning.

Wise reflections are a way of harnessing concentration in the mind. They enable us to focus single-mindedly on the insights that come with wisdom, and help us keep away from useless flights of fantasy. They nurture goodness and purify the inner machinery that sets the course of our outward actions.

The practical application of these gentle teachings is by no means easy. But neither is this challenge beyond your abilities, or anyone else's, for that matter. You can start this process at your own pace by first concentrating only on thoughts that draw your attention. Then, ponder all ten reflections at the end of the series with great care and deliberation, taking time with each of them. Any one of them can be your teacher. Persistence and patience in this practice will eventually and surely yield untold blessings in many, many ways—ways that you cannot even begin to imagine. Cultivate this opportunity with diligence. You may find that it is just the catalyst you need to transform your life into one that is worthy of your noble intentions. You know that you are a lot better person than your speech and actions suggest!

Take this offering of spiritually energized thoughts, and sow them in your mind. Watch them grow and take root in your heart. Let them work in you as they were intended, bringing you to openness, instilling in your heart the knowing bliss of calmness, and leading you ever closer to perfect peace.

REFLECTIONS
FOR THE HEART

❖

Life is endless. We are all in the very middle of it. We alone are responsible. There is no way out except through it. At the same time, your life is exactly what you need to unravel your karmic predicament. The teacher you seek to lead you out of your suffering is within you.

All religions are identical in their aspirations. We can dispense with everything involved in ritualized religion simply by listening carefully and following the still, sensitive, compassionate, virtuous inner guide. Be still and know the life within. Do good, refrain from evil, and clear your mind of unworthy distractions.

The all-in-one God, or dharma, is every-thing and no-thing simultaneously. Because this concept is unfathomable and beyond our rational comprehension, we resort to calling it God. It is the single energy capable of orchestrating and energizing this unfathomable world. It also creates the illusions that hide its presence from all but the most sensitive and diligent. It is this aspect of creation, the dance of the *samsara,* the endless cycle of birth and death and birth, that makes our existence so intriguing.

If you have been too distracted to have any contact with this subtle, sensitive energy, try to lighten up your life until you can tune into this "suchness" at will. When you get out of the way, this energy just flows. You merge with the flowing. Practice diligently and you can keep the line open so that all sorts of interesting messages can come through at any time. Reduce tension, relax, eat light foods, wear natural, light-colored clothing, be with good friends. Choose only companions who delight in supporting your spiritual development. These skilled habits will enrich your life and make it into a buoyant adventure.

Consider this: Everyone, without exception, is in the same boat, subject to similar conditions, challenges, and suffering. How can anyone knowing this harbor anger or ill will toward another?

If you look around you with intellectual and intuitive sensitivity, it becomes evident that we are here to help each other grow into graceful, elegant, loving, and compassionate beings—light beings and beings of light! We are here to serve. To give. To sacrifice.

RECYCLED WORLD

Not only is this world round, as Galileo declared, the entire universe moves in a circular pattern. Things spin around and around, and we are helplessly trapped within its vicious, recurring cycle. This means that we don't "go around" just once. We go around and around to the point of utter desperation, until we are disenchanted with everything and go out in search of a way to break out from this hopeless, hapless situation.

Whether you are lying on a beach in Hawaii or doing time in San Quintin, this world remains a cage. We live driven by our karma. Under the influence of culture and karma, we live different lifestyles, but we live them always within a cage. Being unaware of our predicament does not alter our reality.

If there weren't an intelligent and tested way to escape this cycle of life, everything would be absurd. And, at least in my opinion, there would be (in the ultimate sense) nothing worthwhile to do. We would be destined forever to live as we do.

But the nature of our predicament is made perfect by requiring us to understand it truly and thoroughly. This understanding spurs us further to seek a reliable and scientific path that offers the possibility of arriving at the exit door that is the gateway to enlightenment and freedom.

If you have a knack for fascinating dilemmas, you will undoubtedly appreciate the ingenuity of the maze that is our world. And that maze is just as difficult to transcend as you imagined it to be. The path that leads out of the maze is the one that follows both our spiritual inclination and the laws of nature. So, by design, we are already programmed to seek a way out and to make good our escape.

Because we have seen the entirety of this situation in our previous lives, we can now appreciate the justness and fairness of it all. We are only obliged to clear up our mistakes, and to do the best we can from then on, continuously refining and purifying as we go.

In other words, we need only be aware and respond properly to every situation that life places before us. With this wise thought as our guideline, we can strive to act morally, intelligently, sensitively, and compassionately.

We are born into this life with a specific, assigned task that each of us must carry out in his or her own unique capacity. The karma that generates life obliges us to purify these challenges and encounters. Our role in relation to others is to be someone who encourages them to do the best they can from where they are, without expecting them to change. We can also try to be a positive influence on others by leading a life imbued with awareness.

A Chameleon Called Self

---❖---

Many of us relate to other people for most of our lives without ever really looking at them deeply and carefully. Has it ever occurred to you, for example, that people, from a scientific point of view, can be described as simply an assortment of bones and organs held together by skin? Furthermore, our entire physical structure, from the moment of birth, embarks on an aging process that gradually ends in disintegration. No one is exempt from this process. Looking at life from this perspective, we can see quite clearly that everyone is enamored of a situation that actually carries a death sentence.

It is important for us to be conscious of this reality all the time, because this penetrating insight that allows us to see through the haze of attachments called self, can provide us with our escape route to freedom. The self is a chameleon that adapts to anything in order to survive. It is protected by layers of tightly held beliefs that, when tampered with, produce fear as a defensive reaction.

The notion of the self as we know it, is actually a deceptive construction known in Buddhism as "kilesa" (Pali word for defilement). Kilesa is further composed of compulsions, fixed attitudes, predilections, cravings, reckless addictions, and all the seductive things that reinforce and reestablish the existence of the self. There are almost uncountable variations of kilesa. As we acknowledge the delusion of self, we must also find a way to reassert wisdom. The spiritual method I present here for doing so is called "unraveling." Unraveling is the opposite of accumulating. It is letting go, abandoning, releasing. In the resulting void, you come up with what you have been seeking your whole life: contentment.

Much of what we believe today has been corrupted by several decades of an overindulgent and demanding "American Way of Life." Only those with sufficient mindfulness can really see the looming problem in this situation. Economic success among nations and individuals does not equate to genuine, lasting happiness and contentment.

High hopes for the future have been invested in this much-touted lifestyle—one that is expected to usher in another golden age. Underneath it all, however, there is a constant yearning for the return of an era when stress and anxiety were the exceptions rather than the rule. Those "good old days," combined with the high-tech, convenient, laid-back lifestyle, constitute an American dream that hasn't quite happened yet. These mediocre aspirations are not worth the trade-offs attached to them: discontentment, crime, war, chaos.

Cool Heart, Wise Heart

---❖---

The world of distraction spins around and around, while moving continuously to keep itself amused and entertained. It transports us to a world of fantasy, or a world of controversy, or competition, or of just about anything other than the one true existence that is right before us. Distraction keeps our heads turned in the direction of momentary pleasures, excitement, and delight. On the other hand, the cool heart, with its spiritual energy, is the sobering factor that keeps us focused on worthier goals. It tempers the euphoria of petty fun. It settles us firmly down on Earth, grounding and sobering us with a clear view into life's many facets in a balanced manner. The cool heart is unmoved by the intoxication of the world. The wise heart is the cool heart. It directs us to a profound state where we are liberated from the burden and stench of self-consciousness. Nothing can be better than that.

MANIFESTING THE IMPOSSIBLE:
Affirmations for Transforming Life

We must strive to do anything that can make the impossible and miraculous possible. A whole realm of good things opens up for us if we adhere to this way of thinking. *Life is made for aspiration and for manifesting the impossible.*

The following set of affirmations go right to the essence of this, to the sum and substance of inner transformation. If you have any time at all in your life that you want to devote to spiritual discovery, I suggest that you work with any of the following affirmations. When you realize that the profundity of any of them can radically alter your relationship to life, you embark on the best of all ways.

Jot down these thoughts on a notepad or card so that you can carry them around in your pocket and refer to them when you need to connect with reality. Keep them close at hand until they become a part of your thinking process. Once they settle into your mind, they can positively influence the flow of your life.

- Life functions on many levels. If you choose to live on the comic-book level, your life will be without subtle refinement or poetry.
- The quality of your life totally depends on your relationship to wisdom.
- Look at life carefully and sensitively. Contemplate the challenges in your life that await your attention. These are the things you avoid or tend to set aside. These are the fears that lurk in the recesses of your mind and lie concealed there in the background.
- Meet the challenge! Do the difficult! If you can't find anything difficult to do at a particular moment, try brushing your teeth with the opposite hand. *Avoid the easy.*
- If you really want to resolve problems well, you must sit on them patiently until the solution pops up. Process them. If it doesn't pop up or process out, then

it isn't your problem and there is nothing more to be done. And you can do that "nothing" with confidence.

❖ Patience is the greater part of problem solving and action is the lesser part. We usually get it backward.

❖ By continually putting yourself in the present, the future sorts itself out now.

❖ Focus your heart on the big problems. The small problems will then take care of themselves.

❖ It's not just cigarettes that are spiked to create addiction, but many other things that we consume in our daily lives, such as the TV news, ice cream, and rock hits.

❖ Silence is a great asset. If you don't have any silence in your life, be kind to yourself and make some. Silence is a form of mercy.

❖ The best medicines are those that work gradually to restore the original balance of your body, such as herbal remedies and homeopathy. Medicines that are formulated to kill the problem end up overkilling it. Nature won't tolerate this mode of problem solving; it presents the same situation in another form.

❖ Illness is more of a warning than a problem. It is a signal that something is out of harmony.

❖ Introspection will tell you what's out of the ordinary. This is the intelligent and sensitive way to approach illness.

❖ The future is built on our hopes and aspirations. Any resolution or determination that you make can be realized in the future. You can experiment with this idea by resolving to quit a bad habit for ten days. Every conscious moment during those ten days reinforces your resolve. On the tenth day, investigate this situation from all angles and note what has occurred. You can use your discovery as a stepping-stone to meditation and a path to the best possible aspiration.

* Difficulty is relative. Only your mind makes the worthwhile appear to be beyond your capability. This is almost never the case. The same difficulty that may depress some is a piece of cake for a wise person. All things are relative to your state of mind.

* On the one hand, there is intoxication of one sort or another. On the other, there is despair and depression of one sort or another. There is, however, a middle track. When you find that track and direct your life along it, it becomes broader. Life, unexpectedly, gets better. Moderation and balance honor your lifestyle.

* It is shocking but true: Each one of us has received a death sentence.

* The less you take things personally, the more detachment and coolness you will feel.

* Be modest. Make yourself available to receive what is given. In this way, you will always be grateful and content with whatever you have.

* Always keep to yourself in a mindful and reflective manner. This stance will put you directly into the hands of the universe. Then you will get exactly what you need at precisely the right time.

* Cherish your life as a process. The results of your actions will take care of themselves naturally. Through this mode of being, you will develop poise, gratitude, and dignity—a quality life.

* The manner in which you carry out a deed is more important than the actual deed itself. It is the driv-

ing force that determines the consequences. Assuming this kind of posture inclines you toward a deeper education—a path of wisdom and compassion that is far superior to any curriculum that any school can offer. The way we do anything is the way we do everything.

❖ Aspire to go beyond the ordinary.

❖ If you don't do good, who will?

❖ Can you be as happy when things are just "okay" as when life is "on a high"? If you can, you've passed the course.

❖ The mind is a vital, living "thing." It can be transformed to everyone's advantage. When you understand the point of human existence and recognize the worth of the tools available, you will be able to expand and integrate yourself at an accelerated rate.

❖ Leave everything better than when you came upon it.

❖ Be mindful of "over-thinking." Excessive thought leads to utter confusion.

❖ Follow your gut feeling about what is right and do it!

❖ Do what you need to do with a willing heart and with all the energy you can muster. This is the way to do things well.

❖ A wake-up-your-life technique: Find your ears and pull on the lobes three times, squeezing and pulling vigorously. This draws energy into the brain and consciousness.

❖ It is said that to be no one and want nothing is to be everything. Life is long enough for us to investigate this possibility. If this is true, it turns every notion we ever had inside out and presents us with an exciting, brand-new world.

* Meditation is not just sitting with your eyes closed. It should continue when your eyes are open. Awareness of reality should become seamless. Eyes closed. Eyes open. Each action supports the next.

* Future plans are fabrications built on banana peels. Instead, cultivate in the present an effort to do your best without expectation. Just resolve to be at peace with whatever comes up in the windows: be it cherries, oranges, bars, or the jackpot. Accept the possibility of change in any direction.

* Everything—E-v-e-r-y-t-h-i-n-g—changes. All the time.

* The best buys in this world: flowers, candles, and incense.

* Make your body a harmonious organism. Keep it well by nurturing it with healthy food.

* Unplug yourself from that which drains your heart energy. You may choose to think about this in terms of your "soul." But in the Buddhist reality, it is soul, as in "soul food," rather than an ongoing alias of who you now think you are.

* Put yourself in the blessing mode. Sit in your center where everything is balanced. Radiate.

* Your center is the center.

* Kindle the world with your holiness.

* Don't get stuck anywhere. There is no need to feel stuck in traffic. Use all your opportunities to your advantage. Traffic jams offer us increased personal time and reflective time. Actually, it is a gift. The red light is our ally. If the world were all green lights, we would have run ourselves off the edge by now.

- Peace means no trouble. Period. If you go peacefully, there won't be any trouble.

- Take five deep breaths and you will reconnect yourself to the real present. Five deep breaths can take you out from under any heavy situation. In extraordinary circumstances, five deep breaths can disentangle you from a problematic world, lifting you to a plane where you can simply observe things rise and pass away.

- Everything that is ubiquitous is addictive. Try to find something that is not addictive in an airport gift shop!

- Five things to encourage awakening: don't take things personally; all situations are really lessons; be a student to every moment; exceed your patience barrier (feel the distress of impatience); listen to silence.

- Subdue the fear of death until death is afraid of you. Fear of death is a cultural implant.

- It is obvious that we have the opportunity here and now to do whatever we want. However, there is a big catch to this illusory freedom. Mistakes do count. Later on, maybe two or three minutes later, we have to pay for our mistakes.

- The harder you drive your life toward money and security, the harder it is to get enough of it. You never get enough of what you don't need.

- Bowing and kneeling are important basic rituals. These gestures characterize a life lived fully, in humility, and in the gentle flow of grace. Practice the bowing until you learn to bow with the mind. This elegant ritual renews holiness and expresses with simple eloquence our gratitude for the opportunity to learn.

- The major trick in life is to establish a symbiotic relationship with everything.

* You must live your life through your conditioned character, but you don't have to act like a character. Life is not a sitcom.
* Immersing yourself in things, situations, or objects is a sure-fire recipe for future agony.
* Life is really more about letting go of things than of grasping more and more. It's about generating the passion to be empty of complexity and chaos.
* Everything is one. Every moment is a recycling of every thought that has ever been born.
* Nothing is far away. We are enshrouded in no-thing.
* The things that fill the mind become lively bait for it. Thoughts arise on their own and serve as decoys for the grasping mind to latch onto and toy with.

The intention of these words is not so much to arouse understanding as to nudge the mind gently toward a more subtle and incisive way of seeing. We would do well to recognize that much of our world consists of the ego-I and of latching on to sticky images. Our relationship with the world is mostly a sticky one. Wherever and whenever we stick, we suffer. The ego-I is not who we are. It is fabricated out of sense impressions and karma. If it were truly us, we would not be able to observe it. The ego-I wants to pull things to itself and own them. This process takes place in our own mind without our authorization!

Everything that goes on does so through the prism of awareness. Make careful action the continuous object of your awareness. Intentional awareness moves us and places us in the forefront of our work. This occurs as we see what needs to be done in any given situation. We must place carefulness above intention. Carefulness needs to preside above all our activities and cradle us within the present moment. Carefulness carries the ethical quality that makes for gracefulness and beauty.

Doing the next thing that comes before you is the easy way to success. Don't make a problem out of life and don't be ensnared in doubt and procrastination. Just go in there and do it. Observe all the minute particulars, and then realize the essence of it. Then let go immediately so as not to get stuck anywhere. Learn as you go.

The beauty of spiritual qualities is that they bring forth much more than dry intellectual tolerance; they infuse loving kindness into all our relationships. There is nothing better than that.

We must say "no" firmly to some things—for instance, old bad habits, and doing things to please and to be liked. Say "no" and you will like your sense of self better.

When we act out of self, we create a sequence of melodramas titled, "A Case of Mistaken Identity." If you look deeply into anything long enough, think about it, and utter its name, its apparent solidity collapses and deflates and then everything about it seems absurd!

Things exist in form only as long as the underlying sustaining qualities support it. The mathematician would tell us that a condition exists in any future "next moment" according to its probability. This is an interesting and accurate approach to truth, as well.

In a general sense, the term "middle class" is a synonym for low-security prison. This state of captivity is made acceptable by trappings of (mostly) pathetic pleasures. But it provides neither time nor space to be in touch with our inner source. Unless we look at the

---

world from an entirely unfamiliar angle, it is impossible to see the haze that enshrouds us in our stagnation. Familiar means "dead."

The materialistic world owns most of the evocative words like love, ice cream, cookies, buffet, sex, and rock'n roll. We have to reinvent and reclaim our holy vocabulary.

Wisdom—
Our Birthright

The Wisdom of Wisdom, or Don't Sell Wisdom Short

❖

Our success in coming into wisdom depends entirely on how well we cultivate the supporting conditions and environment for its growth. The conditions I refer to are the skillful actions and responses that we, as maturing human beings, are capable of generating. It is precisely and only at this point that we can determine the actions of our body and speech (we can't control the mind very much) to have either a positive or negative effect on the people around us. As thinking human beings, we can choose not to act and speak in a manner that is demeaning or shameful. Our natural proclivity for righteousness, or the ability to feel shame, can become our guide in behaving harmlessly and in harmony with other beings. Without it we would be untethered and absolutely free to act selfishly and destructively with impunity.

Because we are endowed with a sense of shame, morality has significance to us. In Buddhism, a moral person is one who embodies the five basic precepts:

1. Refraining from harming any living being.
2. Refraining from wrong speech.
3. Refraining from sexual misconduct.
4. Refraining from taking that which belongs to others.
5. Refraining from intoxicants and mind-altering substances.

This code of ethical conduct serves as a guidepost in the development of wisdom. By training our hearts and minds to live within these guidelines, we become less and less inclined to step beyond them. For instance, the simple act of refraining from drinking—even just a sip of wine during celebrations, as at a wedding, when such an indulgence is considered acceptable or even expected—provides a positive statement of graceful restraint. But more than that, it reinforces conscious behavior and makes us less open and vulnerable to the same temptation when the next, less auspicious, occasion arises. Although indulging in modest drinking hardly constitutes a crime worthy of condemnation, this type of habitual behavior, based on ignorance, inhibits the emergence of wisdom.

It is only through diligent, consistent, conscious living that we eventually open up to wisdom and allow its tandem virtue, compassion, to unfold in our hearts. These are the highest male/female energies of which we are capable.

By strengthening and building up this foundation with skillful deeds and thoughts, we begin to encourage concentration in our minds, bringing about heightened clarity and alertness. Our memory expands to keep us from repeating our mistakes. We begin to feel more grounded, more centered, and less susceptible to the invitations of petty diversions and modern, sophisticated advertising ploys. If, with our growing concentration, we still fall short of our goal of attaining wisdom, we will have come a long way toward calming our spirit and bringing into our lives the desirable qualities of tranquillity, stability, and peace.

There is a lot more that we can attain through sane living, focused attention, and meditation. We can change our lives radically from a secular, consumer-oriented existence to a spiritual, wisdom/compassion-based existence. For this, we need to apply ourselves in a way that cuts through the foolishness, the pettiness, the superficial chatter and selfishness of our everyday lives.

The reflections that are sprinkled throughout this book are designed to invigorate the mind, and to prod it onto the path of awakening. This is one of the most effective tools we can use to support this process of transformation. It is probably the best way for people engaged in a busy lifestyle to grasp something that reminds them that life is deeper than the conventional reality. Life is deeper than verbal language and optical images.

In a culture whose primary means of communication is verbal, we, who were raised in it, use words quite naturally to think, plan, motivate, and propel us through our daily lives. These very words, however, can become useful contemplative devices that can lead us behind and beyond their own facade to a way of comprehension in which wisdom rules the moment, and all our ideas, judgments, views, biases, prejudices, and preferences become secondary. This is a way of wisdom through which wisdom itself becomes a lifestyle—a manner of living grounded in the center of the present moment.

I notice that the people genuinely interested in the path of wisdom are those who desperately yearn for change. Having looked deeper into life, they have come to recognize its inherent problems and seek a way out of its tangled web of conflict. This soul-searching process is, already, wisdom in action.

When we investigate life objectively, we will see that it is one immense and frightening mine-field of difficulties and traps. The life of a human being, with all its endless variations and permutations, is a constant struggle—from its first breath as a newborn infant to its final moment, when the last breath is breathed out and no more breath comes in to replace it. As we are already born into this world, or better put, forced into it by our karma, we are obliged to pursue this life to the best of our ability.

While some of us may not have the need to struggle physically and financially to survive, all of us still have to contend with daily psychological battles. It is this struggle that brings us most pain. We can endure the suffering of external poverty, shuffling along from day to day on the streets of some city, as long as we have friends to sympathize with our predicament. The inner hunger, on the other hand, we must suffer alone. The friendship of a million people can not eradicate it.

It doesn't take a university education to land in this neurotic state. Although it is commonly known that most people who have spent several years in pursuit of this so-called higher education are the likeliest victims of chronic psychological distress. Not many of us can claim that thoughts of suicide have not crossed our minds from time to time, especially during periods of extreme emotional stress. Such drastic thoughts result from an unremitting buildup of frustration, disappointment, confusion, and chaotic life situations. Sadly, suicide has now become a realistic "option" for all classes of people in industrially developed countries. Why? Because, as we accelerate the pace of the world into a mad spin, we are thrown into a vortex of hopeless, complex situations and utter confusion. Most of us choose to ride it out. If we do so aimlessly, without hope of escaping to a refuge, and with no vision beyond what we see in newspapers and on TV, we are doomed to an impossible, meaningless task.

Typical middle-class citizens coping with life in a modern society face the burden of making hundreds of decisions and choices every day. Just surviving through a few hours of shopping at the mall or mega-supermarket, or dealing with all the compromises required to manage their lives often dampens their enthusiasm for exploring life in a fuller, deeper manner. By the end of the day, they are thoroughly exhausted from this struggle and can only hope that sleep will provide the much needed respite. But the unresolved "stuff" of the day continues to spin throughout the night requiring decisions and compromises that, in turn, demand even more decisions and further compromises. In spite of all these transactions playing through the mind, there remains an underlying dissatisfaction—some lingering feeling of disappointment—as these people discover that they rarely get what they want, seldom do exactly what they want to do, and almost never are just who they want to be. Often, they end up getting just the opposite of what they want.

Another issue that continues to bewilder most of us (and, I suspect, will continue to do so for a very long time) is relationships—an immense field of suffering in contemporary society. Somehow, we are always caught off guard and ill-prepared to handle the intricacies of this unique human experience. From the difficulties and problems we encounter in our daily relationships, we get an inkling of how extremely delicate and demanding human partnerships can be. Although we can never have all the answers in this lifetime, with wisdom, we, at least, can begin to understand the dynamics of this complex system, and apply in our behavior toward our partners, the key virtues of patience, forgiveness, and acceptance. From there, we can expand the scope of this understanding to include other relationships—with our children, our parents, our siblings, in-laws, and ex-spouses, our associates, the boss, and our neighbors.

As if this were not enough, we still have to cope with the whole agenda of safety and security. Will there be enough money for the children's education? The car is getting old; the braking system is outmoded; it has no air bags; it doesn't look good anymore. The neighborhood is becoming more seedy and dangerous. Then, there are job concerns of downsizing, cost-cutting, mergers, layoffs, and redundancies. What to do? Where to go? Behold—the headaches of planning a future in a world of inherent uncertainty!

The demands of the Plastic Age are as mind-boggling to a generation X-er living in the fast lane in New York as they are to a retired pensioner planting bougainvillea in Florida. A built-in gamut of problems regarding money, taxes, politics, relationships, security, health, and hundreds of modern-day concerns perpetually assault the mind, causing people to have headaches, backaches, and all kinds of other aches. These are simply the inherent and unavoidable peculiarities of a modern, urban life.

As inhabitants of this world, we come into it saddled with severe disadvantages. Once our minds recognize these dilemmas, they promptly shift into a system of neurotic whiplash reactions, jumping hither and thither, hardly ever finding a place to rest and recover. This hot, jumpy mind stumbles constantly from one trouble to another, without respite, out of control, saturated with sensual desires, ill will, fear, anger, and juvenile demands. If we could but listen to this mind with a stethoscope, we would hear it whining, "I want this, I want that, I want to be this, I don't want to be that, I want more status, love, respect, praise, adoration . . . I want everything, NOW!" This destructive, chaotic behavior of the mind can push us irretrievably over the edge of sanity—which is why Prozac is now one of the planet's most prescribed drugs.

We have to strengthen and purify our minds by bringing space and silence into them so that they don't get swallowed by this continuous on-rushing self-concern. Our habitual confrontational stance, combined with karmic conditions, leaves us depleted of our natural wisdom. A mind locked in perpetual thought and decision making falls into a sand trap un-til its natural, alert radiance all but disappears. This happens so gradually that we hardly even notice losing it.

Without this faculty of wisdom, we will find ourselves adrift in the darkness of ignorance, because only wisdom can guide us through this situation with intelligence, sensitivity, and compassion. We are the only ones who can have access to it by direct experience.

29

Wisdom is the energy that can bring about significant change in ourselves. Only wisdom can catapult us to a higher dimension, a wider plateau from which we can view the world of clinging phenomenon with knowing detachment. Without the input of wisdom and the influence of intuitive awareness, no significant change in our conditioned habitual attitudes can occur. The mind, untouched by the grace of wisdom-compassion, can only spin around the same themes, monotonously, to the point of dull stupor. The mind perpetually hungers for wisdom to shine through, but is unable to break the vicious cycle to provide an opening through which wisdom can enter.

The worst consequence of this situation occurs when death sneaks up behind us and overtakes us before we understand the terms of our contract with this life. We then have to "retake the course." Nor are there any guarantees that the next round will be spent in more comfortable surroundings and better conditions. We need only look around us to see the miserable circumstances with which most people have to struggle. The thought of having to relive a life of suffering due to yet-unlearned lessons should give us pause and make us seriously reconsider our present course. What is there to know in this life?

The practice of Buddhist dharma is founded on the concept of knowing the way things actually are. The major source of our suffering comes from the desire to change this. We seem to assume an attitude of always wanting something else—a life in a different community, city, or country, or perhaps even in another era when living was not so harsh and complicated. But even if that era had been an enviable time in our human history, that wouldn't the way it was now. It would be just another chapter in a history book.

The present, where we are, is a complex time in which the ways of wisdom have been smothered by all manner of things and has all but disappeared. We grew up without the guidance and intelligence of mature mentors and spiritual teachers. In a real way, we are survivors of a childhood that deprived us of meaning, vision, and understanding. For some of us, it is only now, as we sit with books such as this, that we begin to have an inkling of what we have always known. Hopefully, this book will be the catalyst for such an experience. It may serve as a motivator to regain an intimacy with the truth.

If all this is beginning to make sense but you are still asking yourself what the downside of this spiritual growing process is, well, there isn't one. You don't even have to give up your appreciation of beauty and pleasure. You can simply take more notice of the limitations found in these and in all phenomena. Refuse to cling to anything that is moving through the passing show. Clinging is an attachment to that which you think will make you happy, but which, with some glimpses of insight into your daily life, you now recognize as the source of your suffering. Clinging sabotages your life.

WHEN A ROSE LOSES ITS ROSE-NESS

❖

Every breathing moment of our lives presents us with the possibility of awakening to wisdom. Every action, every thought we generate leads us constantly to the brink of discovering our true selves. Yet we are kept from stepping into this enlightened state by our willingness to fall prey to the more obvious charms of our material world. Often, we may appear foolish for choosing to sit quietly in meditation, rather than indulging in activities like watching a movie or partying all night. It will take a good deal of effort and spiritual training for our minds to reach a point of maturity at which it is finally able to recognize the nature and subtleties of inner wisdom. As spiritual apprentices, we need a good deal of training and preparatory work. Moreover, if we are determined to succeed, we must also be willing to put forth the right intention, and support it with the right effort.

In your quest for the ultimate peace that is the abode of wisdom, you will do well to undertake some spiritual exercises to train your heart to recognize that great gift that is constantly offered to you in each moment. A good way to do this is by the simple method of reflecting on an object that you come across regularly. Try this simple experiment.

Find a fresh flower, preferably a rose, and concentrate on its beauty. Examine its delicate structure, the velvety, soft texture of its petals, the richness of its color, its subtle fragrance. Do this for ten minutes. Initially, your mind will enjoy this impression, but you will soon discover that even such beauty cannot sustain your attention beyond a few minutes. You will be amazed at how little time it takes before your rapt attention starts to wane. This experiment effectively illustrates one of the most basic laws of nature: everything changes. When you fix your attention on the rose, you automatically operate within the boundaries of that natural principle. This is just the way it is.

So, you sit before the rose, delighting in its beauty. That beauty arrests your attention. You behold the splendor of the rose in rapt fascination, admiring its form, color, texture, elegance, and the rest of its attributes. After a short while, however, you feel the need to shift your viewpoint, because the fascination of that particular angle has faded rather quickly. So, you change your position or tilt the rose at a different angle, hoping to recover the same degree of pleasure that it originally gave you.

Here, in this simple experiment, lies a profound truth—inherent in the arising of beauty is its passing away. BEAUTIFUL, BEAUTIFUL, beautiful, ah, beautiful, ah, yawn, beautiful . . . beauty cannot be sustained. Or more precisely, attention starts to wane because attention cannot sustain itself upon anything whatsoever. That is its nature. The rose remains beautiful, but we are incapable of sustaining our appreciation of that beauty. So, inevitably, our admiration is quickly replaced by indifference, followed by disdain, and, finally, contempt. In a matter of minutes, the cycle takes us through absolute enchantment, all the way to contemptuous rejection.

It is a common mistake to seek happiness in beauty. We often fall into this trap quite unknowingly. For instance, who among us can deny the deep pleasure we derive from just looking at a rose, or watching the iridescent wings of a hummingbird, or receiving a joyous smile from a beloved? It is easy to confuse this intense delight with happiness. But, harking back to the lesson of the rose, the pursuit of such transitory pleasure is like being caught in a hamster wheel. The more we accelerate, the faster we go nowhere.

Still, it is this quest for happiness that motivates our every action in life and pulls us through all kinds of travail and all manner of calamity. As long as hope is alive, we keep reaching out for whatever happiness we perceive as worthy of our efforts. Some of us seek a more refined, loftier happiness and are quite prepared to invest a lifetime in its pursuit. Others look for happiness in more mundane situations, hoping that the quest for happiness will not require too much effort on their part. In either case, this yearning for something better reflects a drive inherent in all human beings. It is the common denominator within all religions. Buddhism uses the word "enlightenment" to designate the goal of ultimate happiness. Most of us begin our spiritual quest, regardless of the religious path we choose, with the secret hope that this will be the way to a sweeter, undiluted, and continuous happiness, without any downside to spoil our fun. This concept is still well within the world of conventional happiness. The wise ones, however, seek a happiness that is independent of the fleeting, changing conditions, removed from the ebb and flow of the moods in our minds, from the quantity and quality of energy in our physical bodies. This is the transcendent happiness that wisdom recognizes as peace. This calming peace does not depend on the absence of unpleasant conditions such as illness, separation, confusion, or even death. It remains steadfast and immovable behind the stage of passing conditions on which all the melodrama of life is played out.

One person who abides in this reality is H. H. Dalai Lama. He lives in the midst of the most barbaric savagery being perpetrated against the people of his country, Tibet. Nevertheless, he declares that, regardless of the unspeakable horrors around him, he is no less happy. Why? Because, in his wisdom, he recognizes with perfect clarity that this is the way things are. He knows that all things, without exception, arise because of external conditions, and that these can only manifest as they must. Eventually, they must pass away.

Thich Nhat Hahn is another notable example. In his quest for truth, righteousness, and justice, he is refused the right even to visit his homeland. And he too recognizes that things occur as they do because of karma. This is an inescapable fact. Only we can combat it through the purification that wise living produces. No one else can bear our circumstances for us, whether they be happy or tragic. But as wisdom begins to unfold in us, we are able to see the rightness and validity of our karmic circumstances, and are no longer deluded into thinking that we have been dealt a rotten hand. Bad things don't happen to "good" people, in spite of what most people choose to believe. Rather, difficult lessons arise in the lives of those who have merited that particular karma by their past actions. We are bound and obliged to learn the lessons rendered by our mistakes in order to refrain from making them again.

The Dalai Lama, Thich Nhat Hahn, Nelson Mandela, and a handful of others deeply recognize that the very life force generated from the mental faculty contains the karmic DNA that create and designate the particular challenges and encounters each person needs to evolve. H. H. Dalai Lama knows that, whether he carries the honor and burden of the Dalai Lama in this lifetime, or whether he lives as a rickshaw driver in another, he is obliged to live out his karma personally. No one else can. In his capacity as a spiritual leader, his most effective and beneficial role in the play of the world is to provide others with a good example. The Dalai Lama, who lives an exemplary life, is someone whom we can all emulate as an excellent role model because he embodies wisdom, infinite patience, and an encompassing compassion that he extends, even to those who torture his people.

The posture of the Dalai Lama in the world presents to us a clear example of wisdom in action. It is wisdom that assesses every situation instantaneously and completely. It functions so quickly that it circumvents the imposition of thought (the past) while accessing an alert, indescribable, intelligent energy utterly removed from anything personal. There is no room for anything other than raw presence. Our personality in itself is an obstacle to present-ness. Wisdom intercepts personality and excludes any notion of a personality that judges itself, doubts, worries, and spins off into any of the numerous neurotic "oil spills" of the mind. The presence of wisdom prevents the echoes of the past and the hopes of a future from impinging into the moment. Where there is no finite self, there is infinite spaciousness that allows the mind to incline only toward noble, elegant, and unselfish actions.

It is impossible for wisdom and ignorance to function in our lives simultaneously. When wisdom is "on," it becomes the predominant force that rules our actions. When constantly sustained and nurtured through daily practice, this benevolent energy gathers even more vigor and momentum to continue its influence on our daily conduct.

Another attribute of wisdom is clarity of vision. This quality enables us to appreciate life's many fascinating aspects, yet, at the same time, recognize that none of these are really worth clinging to. This knowing detachment neither initiates future desire nor tarries in the stale memories of the past. Pure wisdom settles in the mind-moment, perfectly equipoised and unperturbed by the movement of changing conditions. It remains in absolute equilibrium amid the turmoil and disorder with which our sensory world operates. Maintaining this state of wisdom, however, doesn't necessarily mean rejecting pleasure or fun. It doesn't call for the exclusion of things that are pleasant and desirable. Rather, wisdom gives us a lucid, balanced perspective of this fleeting enjoyment that effectively cools down our fantasy-based euphoria. This is the way to maintain a keen sense of proportion that can prevent pleasure from seducing us into a roller-coaster ride of pleasure and pain.

It may surprise you to learn that wisdom is actually the natural state of the mind. When wisdom reigns, the mind stays true to its original nature, abiding in brilliant clarity. Why, then, you may wonder, do most of us exist in a perpetual state of confusion? This comes about through our daily involvement in mundane, habitual preoccupations. Our constant exposure to external conditions and superficial influences eventually blunts our natural ability for intuitive discernment. In such a muddled frame of mind, we are likely to fall into the trap of misconception and delusion. We may even come to accept neurotic behavior as normal conduct, since our impaired inner vision can no longer provide clarity.

EVERYTHING
IS ONE

—❖—

You and every component that make up the universe—
every idea, every atom, every individual being, every
single mind-moment—are parts of one whole thing.
Recognizing this truth is a process of interfacing back
to the source, the origin, the universal consciousness.
Everything is one.

❖ Every atom breathed is breathed by everyone.

❖ Contacting anything within us connects us with everything, everywhere. At that given moment, we may
just be dwelling on a particular aspect of our greater
reality. Most people are compulsively looking, seeking, clinging to these individual aspects. Being with
the whole, undissected world, however, is freedom.

❖ All things exist as a stream of interdependent conditions. Nothing exists on its own and of itself. Everything is related to something and dependent on
innumerable factors. We are all "hanging in there"
together. If someone could be truly extinguished, we
would all disappear as well.

❖ All time/space is interconnected. Present thoughts
arise as a direct result of past thoughts and actions.
Our thoughts in this moment will, in turn, produce
future thoughts. And so it goes on, *ad infinitum.*

- All components of the universe interact and dovetail with every other aspect, so much so that, eventually, we can no longer call them "aspects."
- All things continuously move toward their opposites, which are really just their "flip side." This is true for both the inside and outside of anything. For the inside and outside are the same thing.
- Everything changes all the time, all at once. Most of it re-forms in the next mind-moment, so that it appears to the casual observer as a permanent, enduring form. Every element in life disintegrates immediately. If it is able to, it regenerates its form. It is important, in terms of spiritual sagacity, to recognize that this condition is new, not old. It relates to the old only in the sense that the energy field from the previous *now* moment touched the next *now* moment and gave it the impetus to re-form. If we do something just slightly differently, in a manner baffling to the secular mind, it won't carry on as the same set thing at all. This concept is difficult to grasp and too many words can render it impossible to contemplate. It must be probed from a mind-realm accessible to us through insight and meditation, for the linear/rational mind can neither understand it nor make any sense of it. This is one of those things, like ghosts or tree spirits, that we try to understand through thought-based intellectuality.
- Life is a Magic Hat. From a single source comes an endless stream of things. Reverse the process and all things will find their way back into the hat. The trick is not to get fixated on one single conponent so as to believe that it is actually separate from the rest.

Understanding these truths will expand the heart-mind into an appreciation of close kinship with all beings.

A Minute of Reality

---❖---

Kindly contemplate: The problems of the world are not external. All the problems that we generate in our own minds are not independent snarls and tangles of confusion. Our mind is a part of the world consciousness.

Wisdom is simply knowing this and living in a way that is in harmony with the facts of life. Wisdom becomes manifest in the acceptance and opening up to all conditions. Foolishness becomes manifest in the creation and reinforcement of alienation. Foolishness takes the unexpected out of life. It wants only that a predetermined situation arise and maintain itself forever.

Enlightening the mind is the way to open toward incredible and awesome possibilities. These deeper ranges of recognition are ours for the asking. We deserve to recognize these further dimensions. That is why we are here. And why everything else is here.

It is entirely possible to cleanse ourselves of all the dust and dead weight accumulated over a span of a million or billion lifetimes. It all begins (and ends!) in this moment. Right now. Beginning from where you are now and onward until the melodrama or the soap opera finally ceases.

There is a simple set of principles that can make life run smoothly, simply, and hassle-free. Just follow this rule: When there is something to do, do it! When there is nothing to do, sit quietly and search inside yourself. Use the opportunity to investigate the contents of your mind.

An Hour
of Reality

---◆---

Kindly contemplate: The measure of our humanity is our empathy to the plight and suffering of our friends and neighbors, and particularly of the "others" in the world. This doesn't necessarily mean, however, that we can do anything material about major problems and catastrophes.

Ethnic violence and war is the strategy of animals. Its flip side is "ethnic enhancing," the active encouragement by a government to promote harmony among all the various ethnic groups that make up its population. Ethnic enhancing actively provides an opportunity for people to blossom so that they will naturally enrich their environment and the world.

Here is a not-very-well-kept secret: Human sexuality is a mind-boggling phenomenon fraught with mystery and bewilderment. There are no solutions to the endless sea of problems that arise and trouble the mind when satisfactory sexuality isn't present. There is an ancient Eastern understanding that is rarely expressed in the media's compulsive obsession with sexuality: Anything that can so totally encompass and intoxicate the mind is inherently dangerous. In Eastern spiritual traditions, there is a fundamental understanding that passion that isn't under the influence of wisdom contains hazards that are bound to ensnare the reckless and heedless. Let go of the greedy desires of obsessive sexuality; step out of its consuming fire.

Relationships should be partnerships undertaken for the sake of growth—a growth that goes beyond the original relationship and takes on an unexpected and unique character unforeseen by either partner. Encourage and support each other, so that whoever grows faster can lend the other a helping hand.

Overindulgence, which fills the stomach and the mind, hinders us from receiving anything more. We miss out on many good things through our extravagances. Fullness generates uneasiness, because there is no more room to accept other good things. Excess generates discomfort, anxiety, and frustration.

Turn away from an avaricious lifestyle that can choke up your world. Come into a fluid and flexible relationship with your inner self. Live life.

In this age of prosperity, many people have slid into the trap of aberrant extravagance. We have come to the point where people can call for the delivery of a super giant pizza . . . for breakfast. FedEx it, please.

Meditation finds a vantage point of infinite resource that enables us to see the world *freshly and continually*. This insight can be compared to a number of experiences—a child's first view of snow, a wise, old farmer gazing out on his land from the porch of the farmhouse his grandfather built.

Historians tell us about the fascinating past, astrologers about the future. Spiritual sages tell us about the present moment. This is the most overlooked aspect of the world and the only real part in the matrix of life.

It's hard to communicate the message that one shouldn't get emotionally involved in the world's problems. There is a built-in, basic assumption that emotions are a precious gift intimately related to romantic love, motherly love, and various other kinds of love. This is the rationale for the social acceptance of open anger, hostility, and irritation.

We also endorse and encourage social drinking, entertainment, and news addiction. We assume that these are good and worthwhile social habits, even to the extent that we see them now. The inevitable result is escalating poverty, confusion, frustration, disappointment, and depression. All these assumptions are interconnected and fashioned, sewn together, into an integral belief system that demands acceptance in its entirety or not at all. The alternative is a more difficult choice because it leaves us with nothing to hold on to. Having never been guided to recognize our inner refuge, we fear being left out in the cold. Alone. This is upside-down thinking.

THE ENDLESS WHEEL OF BECOMING

❖

The objective of this life-passage is to find out how to get off the wheel of beginning-begetting-beginning-begetting-beginning. When we figure this out, the result is happiness and peace.

People who have gone a long way toward discovering the nature of this world and who are now poised to end their continuous process of rebirth are called "once-returners" (those who need only come around one more time). Those who have yet to discover the reason for this life-expedition can be called "multi-returners." They will be coming back quite a few more times. When you see the situation clearly, however, the thought of returning even one more time is frightening.

Until we enter into the stream—that is, until we are safely and securely embraced within the stream of dharma—we are nowhere. Here in this limbo there is no telling whether or not we are ascending or descending along the path of awakening. Everything is temporary, since nothing can be secured in a flowing stream.

MEDITATION PRACTICES

PRESENT-MOMENT PRACTICE

❖

The special quality of being in the present moment is that it eliminates the problem of life straight away. In the present moment, *you* are not there. There is just empty mind observing the kaleidoscope within. After all is said and done, freedom of mind, that which arises when the ego-I is not in the way, is the critical "experience" to attain. A mind that is able to be present is unburdened by the absurdity of greed, lust, selfishness, and foolishness. Of course, there is no "experience," as such, to experience, for the perpetually unsatisfied experiencer is absent. It is in this emptiness that all insight and compassion arise simultaneously and continuously. A great light permeates the mind with the realization that we don't actually die. Unenlightened life in all its forms runs around in a circle. Form deteriorates and dies (the four elements: earth, air, fire, and water), but the mind isn't material, it isn't form. It isn't subject to disintegration and destruction. It doesn't die. This is the realization of *amarit dhamma* (that which transcends death). The confusion and fear that surrounds death is finally deeply understood.

The haunting anxiety that plagues the life not-yet-recognized is resolved. Here is perfect balance and perfect centeredness—perfection, not as a static state, but as the point into which the mind is free to incline. Even in the midst of incessant thought (for the mind is a thought/image/sensation environment) there is balance, centeredness, and peace. The ego-I has disengaged and the alluring proliferation loses it ability to spin the mind into a tizzy. The mind (we can now call it the heart) abides at peace. The heart has reverted to its normal state, one characterized by lightness, absence of need, the inner sound of silence, acute inner perception, and other radiant qualities. There is a clear inner appreciation of distance from the captivating aspect of the world, an appreciation that creates a space in which to breathe. Isn't this a state of being worthy of your life?

To find out if it is actually possible to come to normality, you must walk a path of practice. Simply bringing your mind to this present moment will transform every aspect of your life. But to accomplish this, you must relinquish the ingrained habits built upon your abandonment of the present moment. You must go against the grain of habit and the penchant for running off into the future full of plans and hopes. You must stop rummaging around in the past, recalling lingering memories that deceive you into believing that the past is better than the present. Things stored in memory should be limited to helping you find what you need, rather than building illusions and projecting them into the future. The past, when plucked from memory, is revealed as a prevarication.

As with most modern meditation techniques (as well as most of the old ones), you can initiate this practice by sitting with your eyes closed and observing your breath coming in and out. Quiet your mind and focus your attention on something as simple and as neutral as the breath flowing up and then out, and then in and then out. Your mind becomes tranquil and stable. Then, focus your attention on the here and now. You will know what this present-ness is by the absence of all that obscures it. Continually returning your mind to the present is the practice. When your mind wants to slip away, slither into the past or fly into the future, simply bring it back to the present moment.

Your mind in the present moment is no longer under a tyranny that creates ideas out of stale images lodged in memory and induces you to believe in them. Your memory bank, which spins out stale memories, is subdued and, to a large extent, superseded. The freedom gained by letting-go of memory is similar to the sense of freedom that comes when you get behind (or under or over) events—when you are somewhere other than handcuffed to the fabrication of mental phenomena that just happens to be occurring in your mind. This is a practice to be deepened, to be cultivated. The results, you will find, are impressive. Determined energy must be there, however, to pursue this when life is flowing easily, as well as when life is difficult. I encourage you to give this an opportunity to awaken you to a new life.

A POWER MEDITATION TECHNIQUE

This meditation technique cuts deep into the appearance of all things . . . without exception. One of the most impressive meditators in the past fifty years was a poor cigarette vendor in Bombay who stood at the corner of a public toilet selling cigarettes for forty years. All the while, he maintained far more vigilance over his mind than over the coins he exchanged in his trade. By the time he had reached his middle years, he completed the course—he became enlightened. From then on, he continued at his stand and made time to offer teachings for those ready to listen. He never relinquished his duties as head of his family, faithfully providing for their needs. His lowly station in this life was his karmic predicament, carried over from previous lives. It was a condition that couldn't be altered. He had to live within its context and influence.

He attests that he was, except for an exceptional faith and confidence in the meditation practice his teacher offered him, just an ordinary person. This unwavering determination with which he lived his life brought him to full maturity— a true human being, beyond the problems of the world. He knew that his meditation practice was giving him wondrous blessings, so he dedicated himself to it with the same commitment and fervor he gave to raising his family. While in physical, material reality, he sold cigarettes, his mind, however, was simultaneously and continually building strength and clarity. In the end, he broke free.

With this powerful image in mind (and the hope that you have digested some of the things on previous pages), I would like to share with you a technique that can transform you profoundly, whether you are at a vending stall next to a public toilet in Bombay, or the computer room of a bank in Anytown, USA, or the file section of an insurance company in West London. Wherever you are, the situation of your life isn't likely to be anywhere near as difficult as that of the cigarette vendor in Bombay—unless you happen to be a cigarette vendor in Calcutta.

I call this technique B-ME (B-M-E), an acronym for Beginnings, Middles, and Endings. This meditation can help you survive the hazards and dangers of the present, irrational world. A student of mine calls this practice "Crossing the stream without getting wet." When you've understood it, you will see the aptness of this image.

The strength of this practice is that it is equally applicable in the quiet of a monastery as in the clamor of a factory. It doesn't require as much concentration as most other techniques and you can grow into it at your own pace, depending on your underlying karmic energies. In my experience, I have found that it is suitable for all types of personalities and is capable of moving beings through all levels of awareness. It does not require a "greenhouse" environment. With this practice, heavy doubts about the usability of your life-space won't arise and disable your sincere efforts. Any place is conducive of success. Every place is perfect. Perhaps this needs to be emphasized, so that so-called "ordinary people" can really recognize that spiritual practice and spiritual progress are not exclusively for the ordained Sangha.

The path shown by this book has been designed and developed, with this meditation practice at its center, for those who want to use their lifetime to grow to their fullest potential. You are no less able to succeed simply because you are committed to a family and stuck in a job or career. Spiritual life is for the clever, intelligent, ripe, ardent, determined, and sensitive, wherever you are, and whatever your life's circumstances happen to be. You just have to find out how to do it, recognize that you can do it, and then do it.

B-ME is meditation designed to help you survive globalization, downsizing, chemical warfare, and all the other innumerable hazards and dangers of the present, insane world. It is a practice for the world, for it brings you to know the way-things-are, not only in the middle of Manhattan, but anywhere else you might be on the planet.

Right from the beginning, if you really want to see positive results, you must make a firm commitment to pursuing this experiment in order to make it work for you. Indeed, this heroic pursuit will demand much from you. In return, however, it will provide you with the enormous possibility of access to everything of value. You will get more than you give, but you have to offer something of yourself to achieve it.

Just as you would approach a piano with the intention of playing well, so must you gather your resolve and determination to do the difficult. Recognize that this is an endeavor that runs completely against the stream of habits, conditioning, and desires that have previously been determining your path unchallenged. The impetuosity of these reactions and energies have been pulling you along too fast for you to control them.

If you begin with earnestness, you will somehow find your way through trial and error. If, in spite of the apparent obstacles and difficulties of this task, you still go ahead with the confidence that comes with knowing that your natural, inherent intelligence will soon enable you to discover the point of contact between phenomenon and the body and mind, you will understand the B-ME in it all.

Next, settle into the practice and begin to develop it. As this development occurs, you will find yourself intrigued and fascinated by the insights that arise, and by the more skillful way you find yourself relating to the world. Your life will become flavored with the special enthusiasm and unexpected insights that come when your mind is imbued with a profound spiritual interest.

For instance, you will begin to understand the true concept of time and space. You will see the difference between conventional, everyday reality and spiritual reality. You will harvest occasional glimpses of who you really are and what this is all about.

In this sacred exercise (sacred because *you* make it so), you hitch your attention to beginnings, middles, and endings. From this moment on, notice them in all things. All things have them. Anything that arises begins. Having begun, it will move to a middle, and conclude in an ending. That ending will produce yet another beginning. If you want to look for any other sequence, you are free to do so, but you won't find things moving in any other order.

Your task in this practice is to turn the *angle of your inner observer* toward these points. Wherever life goes, you go along, with this awareness as your guide and mentor. This type of meditation pilots your life safely by keeping your inner posture/gesture in touch with the source.

The three points, beginning, middle, and ending, are inherent in all matters and situations, and are the initial insights into the nature of phenomenon. In the world of your practice, you will find that these "points," which you regard as concrete entities, breakdown and merge into one another. Beginning is just a term used for expedient purposes rather than for defining an actual, solid place.

When you study the beginning of things, you will realize their origin and what this insight has to say about who you think you are. When you study the middle of things, you will learn how difficult (at first) it is to pinpoint this particular moment and how everything relates to that which you set up as a reference.

When you observe the ending of things, you will see how quickly this flips over and becomes the beginning of something, that *same* something. The ending of something is the beginning of another thing.

All beginnings, middles, and endings are flexible and capable of shifting and changing places at any moment. It is possible to see, intuitively, that beginnings follow endings as much as endings follow beginnings. This can not be seen through ordinary eyes, but only through the eye of wisdom. This eye we call "insight," or inner sight—seeing something from a totally different perspective from the one dictated by our acculturation. This insight is pure seeing, untainted and direct. It sees beyond the world of symbols and languages, where no secular factors can impeach or alter the view of the way things are.

BEGINNINGS

———❖———

Note that there is a beginning. *What is a beginning, anyway?* Where does it originate? Everything must have a previous or an antecedent cause. This is a causal world, so it has, necessarily, a beginning/s. These beginnings are quite easily observable.

We are prejudiced toward beginnings. We love grand openings, premiers, new cars, new products. We have learned to anticipate the beginning of a movie, a concert, a TV program, basketball games, and tennis matches. Everything begins from something. Babies are the beginning of people (there is also a beginning of babies, and the beginning of zygotes, and the beginning of ???). Weddings are the beginning of long-term, intimate relationships. That first glance was the beginning of the first kiss, which was the beginning of the wedding. All these beginning moments anticipate the inevitable separation. Actually, beginnings and endings should be given equal reverence and appreciation in our lives.

Make a move, any move, and there is a beginning of that move. Let's say you blow your nose, rub your eye, get up from a chair, or open the refrigerator door. The first movement toward the intended result is a beginning. Now, if you look carefully, the beginning of any of these activities actually began a lot further back than the gestures that initiated your body's action. There was first a thought filled with an intention or desire to do something with your physical body. The mind precedes all action. Thought is the predecessor to any action. Think about it. Can you do anything without the thought of what you want to do coming first? Even if you decide to let everything just happen, regardless of the outcome, you still had to first decide in your mind to let everything happen. There is no getting around this fact. Even the marvel of spontaneity doesn't circumvent this order of things at all.

Take a moment to look into spontaneity and notice that this is a special, unimpeded energy. When you recognize that spontaneity is something of a different order or mode than ordinary deliberated thought, you must examine a deeper level of precedent thought to get a sense of the origin of spontaneity. The manner in which a thought-form arrives becomes an object of investigation.

Spontaneity issues one definite, unpremeditated option selected by the intuition itself as the one most appropriate in that particular mind-moment. The beginning of this preselected thought came into consciousness directly from the unknown. Trying to find the beginning of all beginnings is a practice that leads to auspicious wisdom.

When you come to these spiritually provocative places, pause from your primary concern here with "B-ME" and turn your attention toward these subtle, overlooked aspects of mentality. What exactly is evoked, deliberated thought, in contrast to spontaneity?

Deliberated thought comes through analysis and rationality. Thinking, coupled with considering, followed by the contrasting faculties, tests the alternatives by weighing different possibilities and contingencies, then compares and judges them in relationship to each other, along with the desired result. The mind is aware of the debate occurring between rival considerations, both bearing positive and negative aspects.

The beginning of rational thought seems to be on the agenda of ideas and considerations spread out before the mind for examination. Here, the mind attempts to sort out the better choices from the field of possibilities and, eventually, settles on the best one.

It's likely that you will come upon doubt and confusion hidden furtively in the darkest corners of your mind. No meditator can avoid them. What is their role? Pause from the primary occupation with beginnings, middles, and endings to notice what it feels like when doubt and confusion involve themselves in any situation. Where is the beginning of doubt and confusion? Are they in your mind all the time? Are they inherent to your mind? If you look carefully, you will see that doubt and confusion arise from the same source as thinking. If there is rational, analytical thought, there is going to be doubt and confusion. Why? Because choice creates them. No one selection will, or can, be ideal. All have benefits and merit. Can you find the beginning of doubt, chaos, and confusion? It lies in ignorance—the ignorance of wanting things in a particular way and no other, the ignorance of being unwilling to face things that differ from your particular and individualized desires. You must practice in order to see and confirm this for yourself.

MIDDLES

———◆———

Anything that has a beginning has a middle. Some middles are rather easy to find—for instance, the middle of a glass of orange juice, the middle of a deck of cards, the middle of a football game, the middle of a hot dog.

Nonphysical things have middles as well, but they are not so easy to identify. For instance, where is the middle of a thought? Or an emotion? Where is the middle of jealousy? Have you ever looked for it? That angle of observation takes the steam out of jealousy, or irritation, or even depression.

If you always look at things in familiar ways, following well-worn tracks, you will never see them differently. You must take a new tack to come to a new perspective. Where is the middle of the second war in Yugoslavia or Bosnia? Where is the middle of the life span of planet Earth?

We don't care to pay much attention to the middle of things. Only very eccentric people celebrate their "half birthday." Nobody verbally acknowledges being half-hungry, or half-tired, or half-sad. Things at their supposed halfway point don't draw much enthusiasm: half-baked, half-dressed, half-shod. As a meditator, however, you will find profundity here as well, if you look for it carefully.

ENDINGS

———◆———

In a world of beginnings, middles, and endings, all beginnings force an ending. Beginnings push through middles and roll on to endings. And what do endings do? Does the energy of the event disappear? No, it doesn't. It goes on to be something new, re-forming in a new beginning, an endless, inexhaustible cycle of energy.

Notice that all beginnings, middles, and endings dovetail with each other. They overlay and overlap. There is no isolated beginning, no discreet middle, no absolute ending. They all come together in one package, connected to each other like a ream of form-folded computer paper. The more closely you observe, the more amazed you will be to discover that this is all that is actually happening within this world of body and mind, our world. The world is actually just a rhythmic series of beginnings, middles, and endings. You have to see the middle, as well as the beginning and ending of things in order to arrive at truth.

Endings are rather obvious. They are seemingly final moments. We have been conditioned to think that, after the ending, there is nothing else. Actually, things end, yet they don't end. The passing show doesn't stop. Perhaps it can't stop, because it never started. In any case, it goes on: events, people, objects, all combine to support the passing parade, this amazing spectacle. Once things get rolling in this world, the momentum continues. It is vitally important to your life as a human being that you understand this. As the understanding of this reality seeps in, what was once obvious becomes just a particular way of dealing with the world. That tightly locked mental construct that predetermines your view of things loosens its grip. With that release comes a new opportunity to develop more interesting and accurate ways to see the world.

ALL ARE ONE, ONE IS ALL

Our consciousness offers us a multitude of dimensions in which to operate. Each level of consciousness offers us a distinctive set of dharma lessons. When we don't encompass the whole spectrum of life, our lives get fragmented, segregated, and isolated within strict boundaries. Once fragmented, we are in serious trouble. The deeper our habits of fragmenting things, the more problems and more suffering we will experience. We must escape from this trap as quickly as possible. For here, in this pit, our minds have, psychologically, fled from reality. When we are trapped in that private, segregated corner, our minds are intent on creating "you and me," and "us and the other." This takes us far, far from an understanding of oneness, wholeness.

This is painfully clear in politics and in war, where the boundaries between things must be definite. Check the space: white, black, yellow, or red. Once we embrace the gospel of separation, we are primed and prepared to cleave everything into "this and that," and "you and others." We are compelled to accept hard lines and inviolable spaces. We can't allow things to merge easily. We expend a lot of energy trying to lock things off, from each other and from the whole. Computers support this way of thinking as well, until it dawns on someone that the closing down of one thing (as in exiting a program) results in the opening of another thing—even if it's only fish swimming across the screen.

If we remain convinced of the concept of duality and come to cherish it, then there must be war—not just in India, or Iraq, or Afghanistan, but in our minds as well. Continuous conflict, doubt, hesitation, and fear. War. In contrast, B-ME, which focuses on the beginnings, middles, and endings of phenomena, will certainly bring awareness and insight into the mind, along with a growing understanding of the one-ness of the universe and an expanding awareness that all of us are not separate, but rather parts of a completely wrapped package containing everything.

All components of the universe interact and dovetail with every other aspect—so much so that, eventually, we can no longer call them "aspects." This sequence is the whole of the world. Beginnings, middles, and endings are the world. Or are they?

Your whole world depends on your origins. The expectations with which you plan things and generate hopes are colored by your experience and the inclination of your mind. That state of mind, or the influence of character, is what you bring into each moment-frame. It is what destroys the wholeness of things, what disguises their true being-ness.

As meditators mature in this practice and become connected to this place, fear begins to vanish from their lives, until, eventually, they achieve a state that fear cannot penetrate. This is one great advantage that your practice can bring to you.

As you begin to turn from a dualistic state of mind toward a holistic one, one question is likely to tickle your increasingly sensitive and intelligent mind. Why do we draw these distinctions and focus on these narrow angles of perception? One major influence we have already talked about: conditioning and education. The other major factor is, of course, karma. The good thing about the karma of people interested in the truth is that it enables them to understand subtle spiritual teachings, and gives them an opportunity to take their human birth and make good use of it. And this karma has provided us (or most of us) with a suitable place to live where we are free to study and practice the work before us—we can walk the path of awakening.

Investigating the path to wholeness can stimulate our intellect and arouse our energy and concentration, which, in turn, urges us onward, deeper into our practice. These questions arise automatically in the course of practice. By training our minds to be present to the endings (and/or beginnings, and/or middles) of phenomena, we deflate our old ways of seeing things, freeing our minds to see things in fresh ways, just as they are.

Through these insights we automatically enhance the quality of our own lives. We see a more expansive view of the mental terrain of our origins and understand more clearly how we have arrived at this point in our evolution. Our appreciation and delight in discovering these insights reaffirms our confidence in this meditation practice. Eventually, we succeed in using this present life to its fullest advantage.

Sometimes you will experience rapid inner development; sometimes you will forget what needs to be remembered. That is simply the way of practice. Most people stay engaged, remembering some things and forgetting those that are not as useful to remember. Remembering, and then forgetting, and then remembering again is the way of the mind. As a meditator, you are privileged to forget what really needs to be remembered. Then, you remember again, until the-way-things-are is clear and distinct to you.

From the inner experience of this practice, you will garner a deeper understanding of your life-work. You will open up to more and more orbits of creativity. You will discover that what you are doing is not an elective undertaking, but the essential job of being human.

THE MASTER TEMPLATE

---◆---

Understanding beginnings, middles, and endings should compose the entire curriculum for a doctoral degree in life itself. This profound realization merges directly into the truth the Buddha himself discovered. Anyone who looks for it in the tranquility and quietude that comes from within can discover it. We can practice B-ME anywhere, anytime (not just in a sitting posture). In so doing, we continually progress in our spiritual life, even while earning a living and supporting ourselves and our families. Spiritual practice and progress is not just for ordained people. It is for those who want to use their lifetime to grow into their fullest potential.

In this field of practice, you will encounter all kinds of insights that are ever present. You will see that this formula or template fits everywhere. It is the universal cycle. It fits into an understanding of the past and the future, of life and death, of success and failure, and of praise and blame. These opposites are actually the same things, seen from different angles of attention. They are two sides of one cycle of manifestation.

In a more subtle and refined dimension of awareness, you will come to know that things are not different and not the same. Neither this nor that.

"Mix and Match" Affirmations

Allow an affirmation to select you and work with it for three or seven days. It will nurture your heart in the midst of madness. We all have our own predicaments. Find the phrases that will awaken your own intuition. Allow that inner wisdom to come into your mind. Allow these thoughts to displace useless thinking. Give these thoughts room to inform you of the way-things-are. The world is different than you imagine it to be. Outgrow the person you believe yourself to be.

Use these affirmations in moments of awareness as "lemon drops for the mind" (you might want to see it in this way).

* I'm not here for the icing on the cake, nor for the cake. I'm here to find the way out. Accept the cake when it is appropriate, but don't live only for the sweet and turn away from the bitter.

* Ugly thoughts are not really ours—not a single one of them, not even memories that make us wince and intimidate us.

* Many of life's blessings come wrapped in pain. After a while, these blessings-in-disguise will reveal the opportunity they represent.

- It's later than you think. There is just enough time left.
- Not only am I still alive, I'm more alive and kicking than ever.
- One soft thought changes everything. One hard thought separates the world.
- The Buddha energy, or anything that expresses no preference, is the loving energy that won't ever break our hearts. This holds true for the blessed ways of saints and other wise people.
- What do you aim to fill when you eat, your stomach or your heart?
- Conscious eating is a careful and quiet event. Perform this aspect of your life's decathlon sanely and you are well on your way home.
- How far do you have to fall before you get up? The farther you fall, the more difficult it is to recover your tranquillity and happiness.
- Take intelligent risks.
- Not wanting to do something is not a factor in deciding whether it should be done or not. Thinking too much about any decision draws you straight into indecision.
- Most of the time, your mind oozes with greed and selfishness. Notice its effect and it will eventually give way to compassion and service. Defilement tricks you into a mode of self-concern and self-interest.
- Be warned! A life that doesn't progress sinks into varieties of depression. Stagnation is spiritual death. When the spirit is suppressed, it slides into darkness.
- With crystal clarity, you can see that it is your very life that engulfs you. You get stuck, trapped in your

life. The pattern of your habits and your doing confines you in the same patterns. Step back a bit and you will get a glimpse of this.

+ It is better to be alertly simple-minded than to be engaged in a complex job while half-conscious.

+ Take refuge in the Buddha (the manifestation of the highest wisdom) or in another master in the art of living well, for anything or anyone else you adore will break your heart.

+ Feed the immune system and the heart. Don't be concerned with the belly.

+ These days, people are very busy. They are not ready to escape their world of busy-ness. Everywhere, things are designed and structured to keep people exclusively in the doing mode. You must learn to meditate in this context of busy-ness/doing-ness, because that is the way things are. Busy-ness expands to meet all space, and includes watching TV, dining out, and talking with friends. The wise ones use meditation to be on top of their lives. People who maintain a meditation discipline already have the seeds of wisdom blossoming within their hearts.

+ Meditation requires energy, determination, and quickness of mind. It is not intended as a hobby for dull people. Dull-minded people can't maintain appreciation for the abstract possibilities encompassed in meditation. They are unable to work with patience on anything that involves time before its benefits can be harvested. They demand instant gratification in all their pursuits.

+ Desire is like a film director who repeatedly calls out "action," the actors following meekly.

DISBELIEVING
BELIEFS

———◆———

Challenge the limits of belief. As you veer away from your belief system, its credibility begins to collapse, thereby losing the energy that sustains it. Without your authorization and acceptance, it is unable to maintain itself and must let go of its more disposable, outer beliefs. The first thing it is willing to sacrifice in order to preserve its core beliefs (or the underlining assumptions that run your life) is its peripheral beliefs. Eventually, new beliefs, more intelligent ones, emerge to replace those that have been discarded.

The belief system is most vulnerable when we attach superficially to brand identification (i.e., soaps, toothpaste, fast-food restaurants). It is most recalcitrant with regard to those core beliefs that maintain us in our identities as male or female, old or young, English or French, married or single, Catholic or Protestant, mortal or immortal, clever or ordinary, weak or powerful. These it will defend to the death.

Your body has natural energies. Don't try to suppress lust by pretending that everything is ugly. As physical beings, we need to learn how to use this fact. If we don't understand lust, we fear it. We may feel self-loathing for not having wiped it out or controlled it. We must first accept this natural situation. Aversion is akin to hate.

Notice that sexual fantasy is often generated out of boredom. The way to release it is *not to give it a second thought.* We can look upon bodies as a way of abstracting the idea of *asupa* (focusing on the un-attractive aspects of anything, particularly bodies of the opposite sex). *Asupa* brings balance back to the heavily indoctrinated mind. If we observe peoples' bodies from a detached and uninvolved position, we simply see that they are ever changing, unsatisfactory, and not-self. The effect is that we can take notice of both the beautiful and the not-beautiful aspects of things, flowers, animals, and people. In this way, there is no denial of what is, nor any infatuation with it.

The practice of *asupa* calls for a balanced, open, and accepting attitude in investigating our bodies. Without mindful awareness, we risk focusing only on the physical aspect of the form. This can easily turn into an aversion to the unpleasant. The words of reflection used in the practice of *asupa* thus become only lip service to what we still otherwise think is beautiful and desirable. This is just another form of brain-washing ourselves that will not lead us to total comprehension of the practice itself.

The human body is a beautiful form. *Asupa* is a reflection practice that puts the mind into a level of nonpreference: seeing beauty without the pull of desire, and seeing the unpleasant without the push of aversion. This practice was commonly used by our wise predecessors as an effective way of transcending the power of sexual energies.

✦ Such-ness is the bare awareness without the burden of self. The unconditioned is always latent. People do exist, but they exist as a process within pure awareness.

❖ In the course of practice, you come to see patterns. This is the gift of insight that affords us a subtle change of view. Seeing the deep patterns with insight leads us to peace and harmony.

❖ Psychological understanding is quite different from realization of the truth. With psychology, you take different angles on the ego. So you must, inevitably, be involved, not above or apart from the five *skandas* (form, feelings, perceptions, mental formations, and consciousness). There is no abiding entity within these processes; actually they are processes within processes.

❖ Emotions are very difficult to handle. In the old days, people dealt with the problem of wild animals. Now, they deal with wild emotions.

❖ Observing silence at any time of the day supports your efforts to cleanse the toxins from your mind.

❖ Sound of silence: When you turn your attention to your meditation object, do so with sustained, poised awareness, fully open to accept and receive whatever is before you, abiding in the purity of moment, uncorrupted by the sense of self.

❖ Presentness: Settle down into the point between the known and the unknown, a point of consciousness, or the center of the universe.

❖ Do you ever feel lonely? It is hardly surprising. You are alone, in the very center of the whole universe.

❖ With a deepened sensitivity, allow your mind to access a wider range of phenomena.

❖ It is impossible to *have* anything at all without having to part with it someday.

❖ To have nothing, to be nothing, to want nothing, and to give away whatever it is that you don't need is the exquisite state of perfect freedom.

❖ Meditation frustrates your tendency to grasp and cling by creating space. This is called o-p-e-n-i-n-g the mind.

❖ Your heart realizes the reality of the moment. It is not caught in a fantasy dance. To die to the heart means to come into the deliciousness of a pure moment of reality—the deliciousness of a moment of purity.

❖ The mind of a fool says: "Just one last chance." "What's the difference?" "This behavior is natural for a human being."

❖ Everything makes a difference, everything is important.

❖ Gladdening the heart: Think well, feel good. Live your life as a shining example to others.

❖ We all experience mischievous, seductive thoughts. We don't really know how to use our minds, so the images of the world come into our heads and rule our lives.

❖ We think too much and base our thoughts on ignorance and on false premises. This is a recipe for chaos.

❖ Actually, if we look at the world with clarity and honesty, there is no hidden meaning to any of it. Behind the shifts, movements, transitions, transformations, variations, and modes lies reality. Things are exactly as they are.

❖ If you feel any suffering in any moment, you are simply behind or beyond the time. You are not with the moment.

❖ Wisdom stands out against a backdrop of foolishness. Light is seen as bright because it comes forth from a field of darkness.

* Honor the *cadence* of life.
* Direct loving-kindness to yourself, to your feelings, moods, and perceptions. Otherwise, you remain somewhere on the other side of love.
* Undercut the power of anger by seeing it in the present. Look intently into all its aspects and it will lose its power. Discard every layer of anger, look into your reactions in relation to the offender. Why are you angry? What do you wish to do with this anger? How far and in what direction do you want to go with it? How significant is this in your life? Is this anger worth jeopardizing your well-being? Is it worth all the time you are spending on it? The exercise of questioning your way through your anger will effectively force you into facing the realities of that moment. It will also give you the opportunity to answer those questions honestly. At the end of your investigation, you can be sure that you have lost the momentum of that anger and, therefore, have regained control over your otherwise runaway emotions. This is one of the great escapes from suffering.
* Mantra chant—how to relate to everything in the universe.
  "Nothing, everything, no-thing, nothing."
  "Nothing, everything, no-thing, nothing."
  "Nothing, everything, no-thing, nothing."
* You are the center of your universe. This is an infinite universe. When you are in intuitive awareness, you are spontaneous and alive.
* This morning is the end of yesterday. It is the beginning of today, which will end tomorrow, which will begin . . .

* Knowing-consciousness apprises us of the truth.
Knowing-consciousness displaces ignorance, leav-
ing nothing more to remove or transform.

* In the condition of self-absorption, we are alone,
alienated, isolated in a vacuum within our own
world.

* Existence is just an extraction from the void, the
result of which is a spark of particularized, unique
consciousness. This consciousness affixes itself to
material bodies. Particularized consciousness is evolutionary. All particularized consciousness is in the
process of moving toward enlightenment.

* Awareness is always in the midst of wanting this or
that.

* What is the good? The good is the evolutionary
energy in the universe. It is a principle. Bad people
do not get goodness. They are able to acquire material things, power, adulation (the world honors the
qualities of people who are not necessarily good).
As for goodness, there is an underlying principle beyond the apparent world that even the not-so-good
people honor and instinctively respect. This principle
contains such a powerful imprint that whoever con-
templates it with a quiet heart immediately sees the
truth of it.

* Do good, get good. *Goodness radiates and sticks to
people.* This goodness has a powerful enduring
quality that is evident in funeral ceremonies. Good
people elicit loving remembrances. Their goodness
stays on with friends, children, and relatives. In this
way, their goodness carries on after death. Only the
physical body dies; the person's good energies remain, continuing the ripple of goodness.

* Love others to the point that you completely aban-

don your self. Die to your self's interests. Focus solely on your aspirations and observe with gratitude and awe what is left in the end.

* What we ponder is what we are. Upgrade your vision.
* Create a free space that can free both space and time.
* Life is only in this moment. Is there life on other planets? In other galaxies? Answer: if they are in this present moment, there is life there. The question of distance is irrelevant.
* The substance in life comes from the quest for profound truth, from the courage to look into difficult questions and from the wisdom to arrive at profound answers.
* Selfishness is the spawn of evil. It is an energy that knows no limits and imposes itself on the needs of others.
* Move away (psychologically, at the very least) from anything and everything that restricts your freedom. Ultimately, you will find yourself totally free.
* Act like a free being, live like a saint, and, in due course, these aspirations will merge and you will be all these energies. Life is in that freedom and saintliness.
* Bring simple rituals into your life. A ritual is the hallmark of respect, devotion, honor. It is a gesture that defines a spiritual/psychological moment and pours love and compassion into the heart. It is an elegant way of highlighting a spiritual moment.
* Every moment overflows with possibilities, secular and spiritual, whichever kind of energy you bring to life (to the present moment). All this potentiality is accessible in the infinite variety of experience that life presents.

❖ How we experience life is up to us. Happy, sad, mundane, profound, beautiful, ugly, all depend on the modality of mind. The ultimate modality, the one that extends beyond all modalities, is peace. Peace, as in the emptying of wanting. This quality of heart determines the nature of our experience. In any moment, when we have a clear, pure, unselfish heart, that moment will be untainted and peaceful, regardless of external conditions, external confusion, or external chaos. Consider this deeply. This is the primary concern for all humanity.

❖ Happiness, in the television sense, is not sustainable in the long term. When it does fade away, unhappiness takes its place, for unhappiness is the ordinary condition. After a long period of suffering under the weight of unhappiness, happiness bursts in with a fresh sweetness. Then it disappears, only to be replaced by unhappiness once again.

❖ All people suffer from being who they are. The less you relate to that notion, the less you suffer.

❖ Emptiness is the foundation of spontaneity. The emptier the mind, the faster and more spontaneously it functions. The more thoughts traipsing through the mind, the more slowly we function.

❖ Patience is simply the wisdom to know that, by waiting, something better will come along. It is this wisdom that enables you to appreciate those gifts better and more fully.

❖ Our lives are squeezed between unseen forces and, to the greatest extent, the influence of karma.

❖ If you could but see your life from a point on the horizon, you would realize that *your whole life rests in this moment,* regardless of whether you are there for it or not.

❖ Thoughts come, but mindfulness/awareness, like an engaged clutch, just lets thoughts go out on their own without getting involved.

❖ Prepare for separation, for separation from everything is inevitable. Found your relationships on a different, deeper love.

❖ In sitting meditation, come to realize comfortable and uncomfortable states of mind as just that—changing, switching.

❖ Who is it that keeps you in the way of seeing clearly?

❖ The *middle way* is no esoteric, abstract code of conduct. It is exactly the point at which you do the best you can. Here, you walk the middle way. It is the perfect condition for transformation.

❖ Make one wholesome thought arise (MOWTA: this interesting acronym would be a good name for a new auto model or hip-hop dance).

❖ The greatest challenge to all intelligent people is unraveling the mystery of who they are.

❖ Shame is the guardian of propriety. Use it positively. Once you add judgment to it, shame will lead to suffering.

❖ Use life-infusing affirmations to perk up your heart and encourage you to evolve.

❖ Life bubbles out from the quest for profound truth, from the courage to look into difficult questions, and from the wisdom to arrive at profound answers.

The Road to Ultimate Freedom Is a One-way Street

❖

More is not better, it is hopeless. After any initial excitement, boredom will invade the mind and then the craving for more stimulation will agitate the mind until all the pleasure in the world, concentrated into one thought-moment, couldn't satisfy craving. Whatever it is, it's not good enough. Wanting more will not hasten your progress or make you move forward faster toward contentment. Sooner or later, your intuitive wisdom will teach you that the only road to satisfaction is by backing away. Freedom only arises out of the gesture of letting go.

WISDOM
IS METTA

❖————

Where there is wisdom, there is also *metta* (loving-kindness). These virtues are inseparable, indivisible. There is no wisdom without *metta*, and no *metta* without wisdom. A heart unoccupied with the mundane makes room for the power of *metta* to flow into the moment.

Metta is that all-embracing, all-encompassing compassion that illuminates the entire world system, pouring light into every conceivable and inconceivable space, and infusing all sentient beings with loving-kindness. Every being, without exception, shares in the outpouring of this blessing even in intangible ways.

The ability to radiate *metta* is by no means limited to those who, through many years of practice, have reached certain levels of calmness and sagacity. In fact, sending *metta* is something each of us is capable of doing for one another because the very nature of being links us to everything else in this world. As you come to a deeper understanding of the nature of *metta*, you will gain more confidence in your ability to infuse loving-kindness. Soon, this generous act of compassion will become an indispensable part of your life—more satisfying than donuts or bagels.

——

WISDOM IS THE MOTHER OF ULTIMATE HAPPINESS

When wisdom illuminates each present moment, the way to enlightenment becomes a well-lit path. You will see everything that unfolds before you with unerring clarity, and be able to choose with certainty and discernment the direction that will ultimately lead you to your true self. This is the state of supreme happiness, untouchable and beyond all conditions. Here, at last, lies the elusive peace that awaits your recognition.

All of us can find some measure of happiness in our lives when things go our way or when we get what we think we want. But to be happy only during those brief intermissions in life is tantamount to being miserable most of the time. The gift of wisdom is to be able to discover the happiness in unhappiness and suffering, the stillness in confusion and turbulence. The truth of this paradox is that all these experiences are contained in the very same space and time. Happiness and peace don't exist at opposite ends from misery and chaos. These seemingly conflicting states are not remotely isolated from each other. They coexist in the same reality. To really know and understand this is to gain true freedom, because this insight releases you from the constricting grip of delusion. Ultimate freedom is the ability to abide in peace, whatever, whenever, wherever.

If you understand even some of this, you know that there is no need to search for peace. The term "searching for peace" implies going somewhere else to look for it. We tend to look outward, elsewhere, as if peace were a hidden treasure buried in some unmarked spot out in the horizon. The main problem with this perspective is the direction of its focus. The more aggressive and ambitious you are in looking elsewhere, the farther adrift you get from the truth.

Wisdom reveals that every state of mind is contained in one, overarching consciousness. Our access to it depends on that to which we are attuned. Or, we can say, it all depends on the level of purity manifested in any moment. Happiness and unhappiness, wisdom, ignorance, and indifference are all on a toggle switch. They don't arise simultaneously, but they do arise in relation to one another. Flip the switch to happiness, and unhappiness disappears. Flip the switch to ignorance and wisdom vanishes.

Since wisdom is ever present and always accessible to us in every mind-moment, we need only switch it on. By being in that one given moment totally and purely, we tap into it. It seems that we need to be wise to have wisdom.

WISDOM

A 30-SECOND REVIEW

---◆---

Remember the necessity of cultivating wisdom if a life is to flourish. Wisdom discovers the world. It is the energy that counters desire and desiring. It can override and extinguish desire and desiring. It is eternally contented. On the other hand, desire and desiring, if left to their own devices, will devour the entire world, and still be voracious, wanting more.

Wisdom that sees the world with circumspection can respond immediately and spontaneously, because objectivity doesn't rely upon memory. It is unfettered energy.

B-ME Practice

A 30-Second Review

---❖---

If you are working with B-ME (and I hope you are), remember that the three points, beginnings, middles, and endings, are inherent in all matters and situations, and are the initial insights into the nature of phenomena. In the world of your practice, you will find that these "points," which you regard as concrete entities, break down and merge into one another. "Beginning" is just a term used for expediency, rather than for defining an actual, solid place.

Eleven Points of Inquiry

The following thoughts are for people who like to read books from the back to the front.

1. All components of the universe interact and dovetail with every other aspect, so that, eventually, we can no longer call them "aspects."
2. The most toxic and life-stifling addiction is the addiction to the idea that you are who you think you are.
3. The nature of consciousness itself is unthinkable and unknowable. All that we can do is toss up conjecture.

---

4. Today's travel tip: where you find yourself is the best place you can be.

5. In your practice, you are bound to encounter these three kinds of mind-moments: pleasure that generates a kind of self-satisfaction; displeasure that generates a kind of aversion; and the space where there is no self operating, where there is no pleasure or displeasure, just a quiet neutrality.

6. Ponder the nobody-ness of things. There is no one behind the scene. What you see is what you get.

7. Having the experience of a memory vicariously and savoring the present moment, no matter how or what it is, are two very different things.

8. All monks' robes represent a dramatic sign to "stop"—stop the inner chaos.

9. One who is sensitive enough to see the danger of habits and foolish relationships with things and people is a *samana,* or one who is ready to stop the world, regardless of whether he or she dons a robe or habit.

10. Rock'n roll band The Eagles pose a question in "Learn to Be Still" about how do we get out of here . . . how do we fit in. . . . Discover profundity wherever you are, even in the pop charts.

11. Viewing the world from the plateau of wisdom reveals that the world is a fabrication of half-truths, lies, and insignificant concerns, a series of inconsequential, uncompassionate events rolling along toward nowhere.

The End Is Also the Beginning

This book has come into print, not to change your life, but to *transform* it. Radically. That simply means that its objective is to firmly shift your mind and that of other readers onto a track that can initiate a kind of learning that will bring magic into your life. This magic we call mindfulness/awareness, or insight. It is an antidote to all the negative conditioning you have undergone that shrank your mind, and constructed a set of primary binding beliefs that you consciously and unconsciously cherish even more than your life. This belief system is attached at such a primal level that you come to feel as though your survival depends upon the perpetuation of this cultural composite.

Insight and mindfulness/awareness develops a whole range of powerful and empowering traits that are given the space to blossom forth. Insight nudges out blind adherence to our cultural identity and unexamined beliefs that have dominated our attitudes.

Clarity, for instance, displaces confusion. Spontaneity displaces all the roundabout thought processes that make life complicated. Spontaneity is an invaluable asset. It replaces doubt and hesitation. Insight creates passageways for energy to arise in the mind.

It encourages diligence, patience, and persistence. With more energy and more patience, your mind moves into a higher dimension. And so it goes—life flowing with vigor and vitality.

With a complete set of "replacement parts," you can manifest proper and appropriate behavior and are capable of standing solid under all conditions. You have the strength to withstand the intrusion of foolishness and mistake making that wastes so much of your time and creates so many problems for you and others. Kindness and compassion overule selfishness; bridge building comes from your deepened knowledge of the oneness of everything. Separateness and isolation dissolve.

As this radical transformation comes about, there is no need to change your religion or nationality, or to throw out your cultural heritage. All the good things you have learned can be integrated in a greater understanding of the-way-things-are. You need only switch on the systems that give access to inherent wisdom. It is in wisdom, with its transformative insight, where you must take your stand, if you want the best this life has to offer. With wisdom as your refuge, you are certain to manifest a dignified and noble life. In the mind, there is silence and peace and a life not drenched in merely political and economic concerns, a life not intimidated by an uncertain future, a life that can face fear, disability, aging, illness, and even death. All this comes out of a wisdom-based boldness that can meet and deal with any conditions. This wisdom-based energy is what invigorates life and ensures that you don't miss or waste any more of this opportunity.

To have arrived at this point in your evolution, you certainly must already have recognized just how many mistakes and misperceptions have impeded and created obstacles in your life. You will have had a glimpse of how many "important" concerns and questions have, somehow, just disappeared into the back of your mind. This distressing phenomenon has alerted you to the need to strengthen and clarify your mind in order to face the problems and responsibilities of daily life. You have recognized the need for a spiritual practice.

Meditation practice, which has been praised by many of the great men and women of this world, is a key to loosening your grip on the whole mass of suffering that engulfs your life. With meditation practice, you can actually see the place where the senses engage and, most critically, where the self tenaciously clings to the arising phenomena.

This practice takes you right there. You can see where and how to disengage.

From the goodness that comes forth out of your affirmations and contemplations, your mind becomes more and more flexible, elastic, and resilient. This is the motion of the opening of the heart. This is the beginning of the end of conflict, neurosis, doubt, hesitation, and all other forms of suffering. Admittedly, this is something special that is not easy to attain. It can, however, be done.

Why you can't get what you want: The functioning of your consciousness generates dissatisfacion and craving, then craving for more, in an endless cycle. This provides little opportunity for pleasure and relief from suffering to come into the heart.

On Forgiveness

––––––––––– ❖ –––––––––––

Your birth (or rebirth) into the human realm puts you in propitious proximity to your ultimate destination—total liberation. As a being endowed with reflective consciousness, able to access that free-flowing energy of supreme enlightenment, you are equipped, even programmed, to find your way into this state. Ironically simple as that may sound, we are all complex beings driven by karmic forces and conditions, responding and acting accordingly. Perhaps that is why most of us choose to alienate ourselves from the very practices that would lead us out of suffering.

In Western societies, it is more common than not for people to be born into dysfunctional families. The constant strife and conflict to which they are subjected inevitably generate certain psychological aberrations. This predicament provides a template for creating complicated, discontented beings inclined toward all manner of illnesses.

Working with spiritual practices is a pathway toward accessing the cosmic consciousness that can point you toward healing and wholeness. It lets you accept your less-than-perfect family as the necessary material you have been given to work with and helps you appreciate the insistent demands for spiritual fortitude. You would not be here expressing your spiritual interests if your painful experiences, provided in part by your familial relationships, had not pushed you to the brink of desperation. For it is the suffering in your life that has spurred you to find a way beyond its reaches, regardless of what it takes.

The drama of your childhood needs reconciliation. You must heal your resentment for what you may have lacked as a child, for the "raw deal" you may feel you got, for all the variations of anger, unexpressed frustration, and guilt that may have congealed around these so-called issues. Many have been encouraged to accept the popular idea that all your problems come out of your parents' nest. Nonsense. You arrived on the scene full of errors that needed to be rectified. If you could understand the reason for your birth here and now, you could also recognize that you came through your parents prepackaged by previous karma, already out of synch with nature.

It is your own unbalanced energy patterns alone that have propelled you onto this plane of existence. You carry a burden of karma manufactured out of the stuff of your long, long history of mistake making. Your present nuclear family did not originate your karmic condition. Millions (or billions) of previous mistakes have bent you out of shape. You have been, up to now, fundamentally a mistake-making creature. Amazingly, you have managed to get to this point to begin to remedy this situation. That is what your human life span offers you. That is why this short existence you have is invaluable. There is a lot to do, a lot to forgive, a lot to acknowledge.

Forgiveness is a prerequisite to healing. It releases you from the clutches of baser tendencies that cause you to scheme and fantasize about getting even. It makes way for spontaneous compassion to imbue your heart with peace, and accepts a more expansive evolutionary understanding that brooks no self-deception.

Delusion or ignorance is the root of self-deception. It is the founding premise, engraved in your psyche from the moment of your conception, on which you build all your ideas and base all your future daily actions. Among these delusions, two are particularly dangerous, because they are the most prevalent and are, therefore, sanctioned by you to rule your life.

The first decrees that loving yourself is akin to selfishness. This idea is so insidiously perpetuated by everyone and everything connected to you socially that you accept it as gospel truth. You become uneasy with loving yourself, or with giving yourself nurturing time. It leads you to accept the burden of responsibility for things beyond your control, but to reject yourself as a worthy recipient of love.

The second decrees that you are a victim of an elaborate universal conspiracy to thwart every attempt of happiness to find you. You often believe that you are at odds with the entire world, a Don Qixote fighting the windmill, a David battling Goliath. This is the "why me?" syndrome that thrives on self-pity and wallows in the mire of self-righteousness. As the converse of the first delusion, it relegates all responsibility for your circumstances, especially the unpleasant ones, to forces outside of yourself: to the parents who oppressed you, the gradeschool teacher who terrorized you, the PE coach who humiliated you, the friend who stole your fiancé, or the associate who cheated you out of a promotion.

The end product of these delusions is sickness manifesting itself tangibly in your biological and psychological makeup. Cancer, arthritis, diabetes, Alzheimer's disease, and all manner of diseases are simply the manifestations of ignorance. Negative thoughts are as physically toxic to the body as arsenic in the bloodstream. Every thought, negative or positive, is recorded in the body cells' logbook, and becomes a building block to either sickness or happiness. You choose your diagnosis without intending to. You are ignorant about your choices, not knowing that they are irrevocably deposited in your system.

The good news about this life is that we have been given all the solutions to these seeming problems. And we are inundated with clues and hints, some of them explicit enough, that we may find our way unerringly to these solutions. In other words, the dice are certainly loaded in our favor. But we have to cast them. We have to make an effort to decipher these clues to our redemption, and we have to have the vision to recognize the reward of total freedom and wholeness that awaits us at the other end of the tunnel.

Spiritual practices are the road signs that point to heaven. They are time-tested formulas designed to sweep away delusory cobwebs in our psychic attic. They are foolproof exercises that invigorate the mind-heart. They clarify our spiritual vision with penetrating awareness and enable us to see with true insight.

With an attitude of clear awareness, you can learn to relax your grip on negative experiences. You can thaw the frozen regions of your heart that have harbored hatred, revenge, and pride, and allow the free-circulating warmth of compassion to seep into your entire divine being. Suddenly, you are able to forgive. You can begin to mend, to heal, and be whole again.

The sustained flow of awareness in every aspect of your life is crucial to maintaining the momentum of the healing process. As forgiveness is the result of awareness, it becomes a lifetime preventive measure that keeps you from being broken again.

The act of forgiveness is a volitional deed that requires purity of intention. This is the enzymatic element that signals the mind-heart to release all destructive notions that you have harbored from the very first time you took offense. Uttering words of forgiveness alone does not effect healing, unless these words are spoken by the heart in love and compassion. You cannot deceive your way out of disease, nor can you lie your way to the truth. The universe operates on its own inviolable truth that even the most intelligent of creatures, human beings, cannot circumvent.

Finding your way back to healing and the ability to forgive is not as impossible as it seems and certainly not out of your range of capability. There are spiritual exercises handed down by our wise and enlightened predecessors who, out of compassion for those of us stumbling in their wake, have mapped out directions to that realm of healing and wholeness. Meditation—the stilling of the mind—is perhaps the most potent practice among these. It is only through a mind unruffled by the distractions of the material world that you can recognize things for what they are—no more, no less. This clarity of vision will allow you to acknowledge that you, as well as your parents, teachers, coaches, partners, friends, associates, and every living being that occupies space and time in this world, are acting out their unique karmic roles in propagating the evolutionary scheme of things. Therefore, those past transgressions you deemed as crimes against you can be reestablished in your psyche as separate and independent from you (nothing personal), just as you can unshackle yourself from the bondage of guilt. The legacy of forgiveness is peace; the reward of peace is the return to completeness.

Conclusion

As you integrate truth into your life through contemplation and practice, your life develops more and more meaning. Through contemplation and meditation, life is enhanced and invigorated. It is good if you can turn your attention to things that bring balance and focus into your life. When you use your time to contemplate the way-things-are, you can only benefit. When this is coupled with meditation, life is firmly set on track.

Life invariably requires that additional effort/energy be pumped into it—beginning with getting up half an hour before the daily demands begin to usurp the day.

Meditation makes rather than loses time, because, in meditation, you let go of the unnecessary, the stuff that pushes you to be busy and active. There is karma behind you, pushing you along the same ruts. The more you generate karma, the farther you go from your true resting place.

Meditation time is time to rest your mind that may have become dim and wobbly, unable to see clearly, respond spontaneously, or see things all-around, in the way the moment actually is and in the way things actually are. Meditation allows you to generate a facile, flexible mind, as opposed to a fumbling, floundering mind. Meditation reminds you that you are alive. It reduces the influence of the neurotic and superficial and allows your essential energies to concentrate on meaningfulness.

You really have only two duties in this world. The first is your responsibility to the things to which you are bound and the need to work for a living—the responsibilities of the secular world. The second is the duty to work your way out of that world, and not to confuse these two aspects of life so as to lose your sense of priorities. You must not become compulsively preoccupied at the expense of your duty, at the expense of your life.

You must become more adept at being a complete person who lives on the planet under the authority of ethics, under the influence of wisdom, balanced and focused and concentrated in order to enter the flowing stream of compassion. You must have an impact. You have a duty to become a good, decent, and sensitive person who is not caught up in the definitions of those who want us to be like them, or to be less than they are. You must avoid people who are anxious around those who reach too high. You have a duty to grow into a state of maturity and not to rely on others to confirm you. You must not cling to things.

Be simple and don't want things just for yourself. Learn to accept gratefully the bit of pleasure that comes your way, as well as the massive amount of pain that invariably accompanies a karma-driven life. Do not follow habits and reactive patterns that hustle you along the same circle of events and relationships.

Recognize that your life isn't really yours in any ownership sense and that you have a duty to do something grander, to have a vision that is far more elegant than your mere personal hopes and desires. This vision can give you a new psychological strength that will call you to use your time and energy in ways that bring honor and dignity to your life.

Reduce your mistake making, recover your vision, your concentration, your patience and humility. Be persistent and diligent. Cultivate relationships that inspire you and inspire others. Spot the situations that generate problems or the problematic situations. Our personal karmic predicament continually crashes events down upon our heads.

Restore meaningfulness into your life. When you contemplate and meditate, your consciousness opens and meaningfulness takes shape. Looking at the tendency toward globalization, and the homogenization of people and culture, and the consequent loss of meaning in your life, don't be surprised that so many legal and illegal drugs are consumed by people in developing and developed nations. Meaning is continuously being drained and washed out of peoples' lives. Anything sacred is trampled upon and pushed aside to make way for the next parking lot. Over these past two generations, the world has moved into a pattern of homogenization and every one of us is born with the virus. Recognize this, accept it, and do whatever is necessary to counteract it.

This book hopes to encourage you to use this span of time, a lifetime, to the best of your ability, to plant seeds, to initiate a spiritual orientation in the way you live so that you can break free from the market-economy mentality that has seized the world.

You can face anything properly, elegantly, when you meet life where it is, in the moment. When conditions are fresh and joyous, we can delight in that changing image. When the karma and goodness sustaining life is exhausted, we can look death right in its face. We live life wisely and compassionately in the beginning, middle, and end.

INDEX

Ajahn Sumano Bhikkhu was born in Chicago, Illinois. He lived there, studied there, and struggled there, until it occurred to him that there wasn't all that much to gain from winning all the prizes. One day, he bought a round-the-world ticket and traveled for twenty months. After staying on for one year in Sri Lanka studying yoga, he returned to the United States. Over the next five years, he lived in a commune in Eureka, California. In the mid 1970s, he entered into a self-imposed three-year retreat in a meditation center in Massachusetts. Afterward, he traveled to England and became the first monk to be ordained in the forest tradition of Thailand at Cittaviveka Buddhist Center, West Sussex. Since 1985, he has been living and practicing in several meditation caves in Northeast Thailand and among the hill-tribe people of Northern Thailand.

Emily Popp, co-author of this book, is a long-time student and disciple of Ajahn Sumano Bhikkhu. Her efforts in helping to develop this book and other projects are her offering for the propagation of the Dhamma.